GW01403391

This book is to be returned on or before the last date below.

HOW DO WE KNOW
HOW TO
MEASURE?

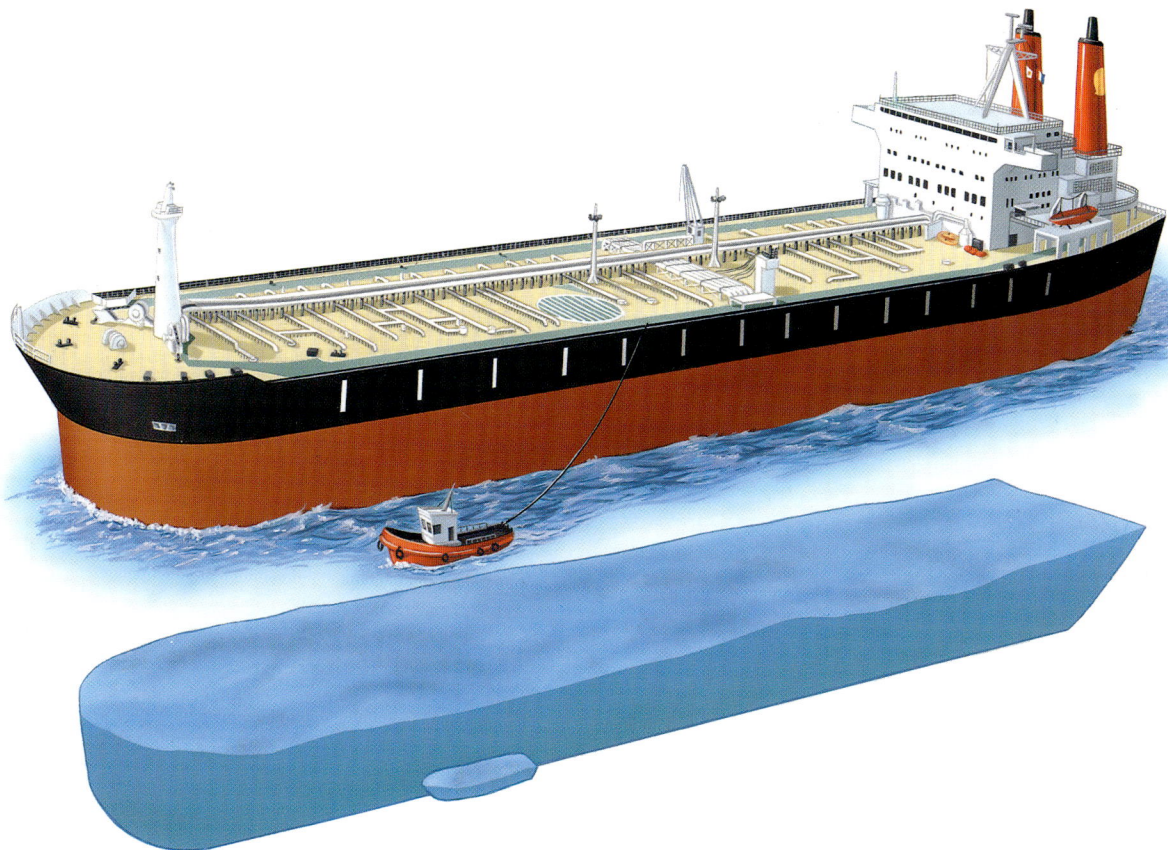

VICTOR OSBORNE

8927

SIMON & SCHUSTER
YOUNG BOOKS

KETTLETHORPE HIGH SCHOOL

First published in 1994 by
Simon & Schuster Young Books

© 1994 Simon & Schuster Young Books

Simon & Schuster Young Books
Campus 400
Maylands Avenue
Hemel Hempstead
Hertfordshire
HP2 7EZ

All rights reserved. No part of this publication may be reproduced, stored
in a retrieval system or transmitted by any means, electronic, mechanical
photocopying or otherwise, without the prior permission of the publisher.

A CIP catalogue record for this book is available from the British Library

ISBN 0 7500 1519 5

Commissioning Editor: Thomas Keegan
Designer: Andrew Oliver
Editor: Kate Scarborough
Illustrators: Mike Lacey, Alex Pang, Daniel Pyne, Rodney Shackell,
Tony Smith and Martin Woodward.

Picture Acknowledgements

Mary Evans Picture Library, 9, 14, 18, 22, 27, 28, 35 top, 38, 39, 42 top;
Image Select 17, 37, 40; The Mansell Collection 11; Science Photo
Library 31, 41; South American Pictures 35 bottom.

Typeset by Goodfellow & Egan, Cambridge
Printed and bound in Hong Kong

Contents

The words in *italic* are explained in the glossary on page 44.

What to measure?

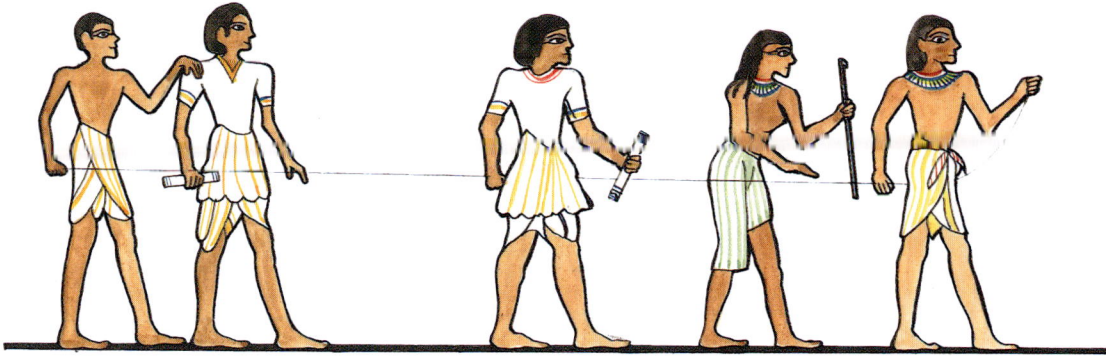

The use of measurements is as old as human civilisation. In fact, civilisation would not be possible without a system of weights and measures that is reliable, trustworthy and easy to understand. Everything that we use is made and sold according to a set of measurements, and measurements help us to understand the world we live in. The first units of measurement were often parts of the human body.

Each unit came into use because it was the most convenient for its purpose, but the same unit might mean different things to different people. The ancient Egyptians needed standard measurements to build the pyramids and find the boundaries of fields after the markers had been washed away by the Nile floods. They began to *standardise* measurements, and some of them are still used today.

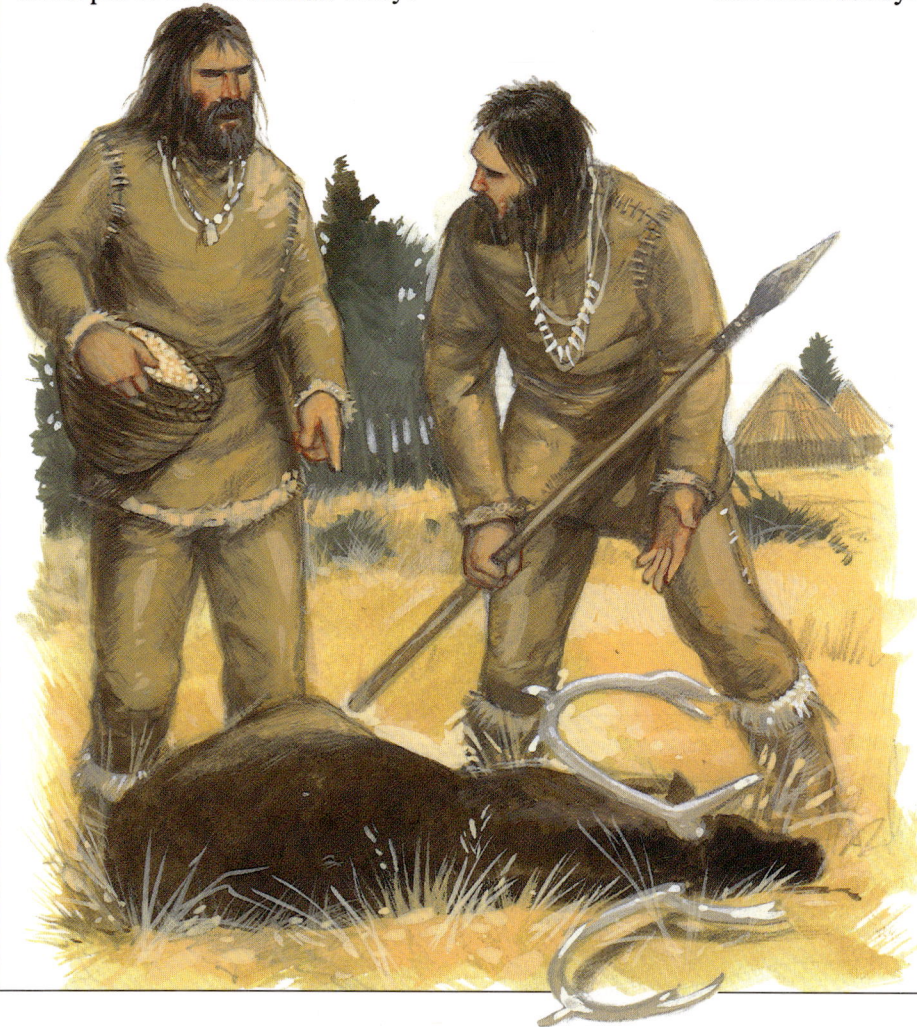

Bartering

The exchange of things is called trade and you do it with money when you buy a magazine, sweets or a bag full of groceries. Before money was invented people traded by swapping one thing for another which they agreed was of equal value. This is called barter. A Stone Age hunter would barter a deer with a farmer for a bag of grain.

Balance of trade

Natural things, seeds, grains and stones we used as weights and measures.

Seeds and shells were also used as money. Precious commodities are still measured in grains and carats (which are based on carob seeds).

Abacus

The world's first calculator was not electronic. It was probably the abacus which has been around for many thousands of years. The Chinese abacus has two beads representing five on each wire above the crossbar, and five beans representing one below the bar. The first wire is units, the next 10's, the next 100's, and on to millions.

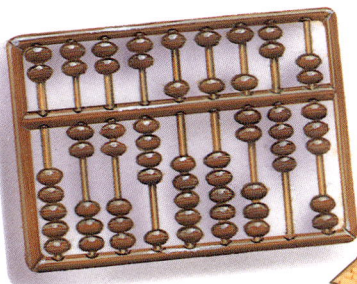

MEASURES FOR BUILDING

The Egyptians took the length of an arm from the elbow to the tip of the middle finger and standardised it as the cubit (53 cms). The Great Pyramid of Khufu was built to it with amazing accuracy.

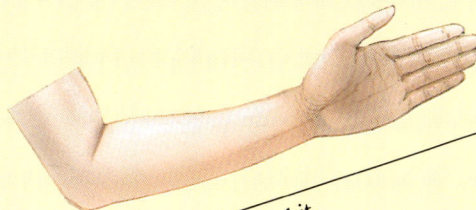

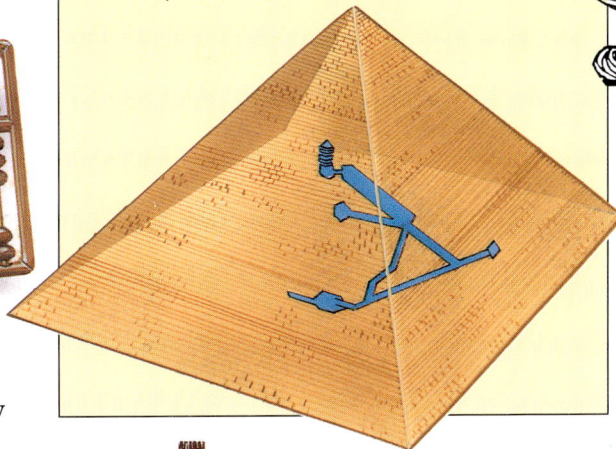

Cubit

Standard weights

Seeds and grains are very reliable as weights, but they're small, and larger natural things, like stones, are not so uniform. As trade developed beyond the simple bartering stage there was a need for weights which were accurate and could be used everywhere.

Watching the stars

Astronomy is the study of the universe beyond the Earth. Early astronomers believed the Earth was the centre of the universe. Copernicus (1473–1543) worked out that the planets revolved round the Sun. Astronomers now use satellites and telescopes in space.

Who's the tallest?

Only when the size of an object is known can other things around it and distances be judged accurately. Otherwise you could be fooled into thinking a distant person was half the size of the closer person.

How long a ruler is?

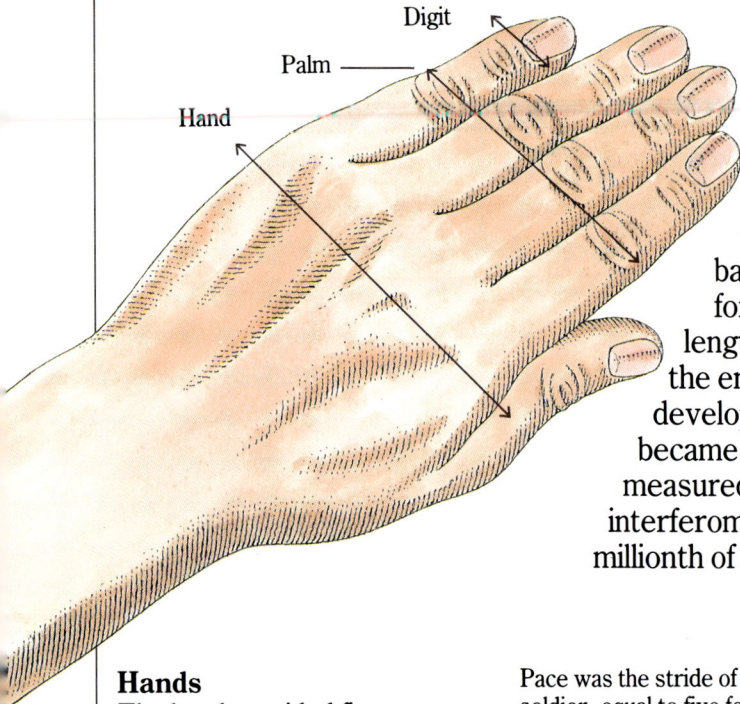

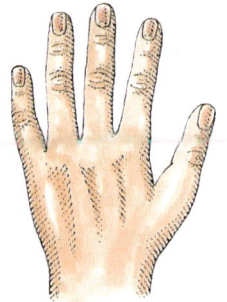

Digit

Palm

Hand

Span

Using a hand or a foot or a step is alright as a rough and ready measure, but all bodies are different. For accuracy these lengths needed to be fixed, or standardised. The Egyptians made rulers out of stone. Metal bars, or yardsticks, have been in use for hundreds of years as standard lengths against which other things could be measured. But the ends tended to wear away making them unreliable. The development of science and industry meant that accuracy became more and more important. Nowadays length is measured against the *speed of light* by a machine called a laser interferometer. Light travels a metre in one three hundred millionth of a second.

Hands

The hand provided five length measurements. The digit, 20 mm; nail, 60 mm; palm, 80 mm; hand, 100 mm; span, 230 mm. The hand is still used in horse trading.

Pace was the stride of a soldier, equal to five feet (1.5 metres).

Step was half a pace, two and a half feet (75 cm).

Roman Standards

The Romans first defined many of the measurements we still use. Their armies crossed great distances, and they calculated these by taking the stride of marching soldiers and standardising them.

The foot was already in use as a measure, but whose foot, and how long was it? The Romans divided it into twelve equal parts called unciae, from which we get inch. It also gave us the word ounce.

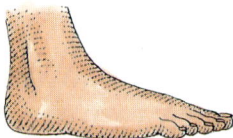

A Roman mile was a thousand paces, from mille, the Latin for thousand.

Measure your foot against the Roman one.

ROMA VII MII

Fathom

Fathom, first used by Vikings as a measure of sea depth, was the stretch of a sailor's arms as he paid out the sounding line, 1.8 m (6 feet)

The yard

King Henry I (1100–1135) decided that the length of his arm should become the standard yard, and metal bars were made to the length. This is how 'imperial' measurements originated. Henry wanted to stop the dishonest measuring of cloth.

Acre

An acre was originally the amount of land that could be ploughed in a day by a team of oxen. This varied from place to place and wasn't standardised until 1824.

Hectare

The hectare is the metric measurement of area. It is roughly two and a half times larger than the acre.

Furlong

A furlong was the length of a furrow (201 metres/ 220 yards) which could be ploughed by oxen before resting.

THE METRE

The word metre comes from the Greek for measure, metron. The metric system was developed on scientific principles in France during the Revolution (1793–1799), and uses multiples of ten. It was decided that a metre should be one ten millionth of the distance between the equator and the North Pole. It was impossible to measure that distance. Instead two French engineers set out in 1792 to measure from Dunkirk to Barcelona. From that they calculated the distance from the North Pole to the Equator and worked out the length of a metre. The metric system was completed in 1799.

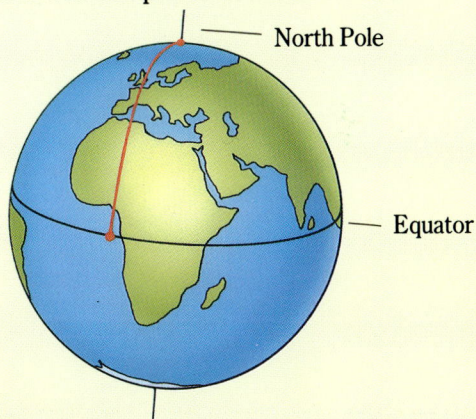

North Pole

Equator

How tall we are?

The oldest known ancestor of humans was an ape-like creature called Ramapithecus which lived more than five million years ago. Our ancestors gradually changed, growing taller, developing more intelligence and becoming closer to the way we are now. We all belong to a species called Homo Sapiens, which is Latin for wise man. It is not certain when Homo Sapiens developed, but they might have emerged about a hundred thousand years ago in Africa. They spread around the world and were living nearly everywhere by ten thousand years ago. Humans continue to develop according to Darwin's *theory of evolution*. There are also factors like better food, housing and healthcare which ensure that people are bigger than they were even a hundred years ago.

Sarcophagus

A sarcophagus was a coffin which resembled the dead person inside, so it shows how big people were thousands of years ago.

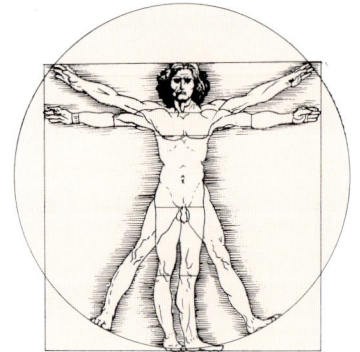

Leonardo

Leonardo da Vinci (1452–1519) believed that mathematics held the key to painting. In his *Vitruvian Man*, Leonardo fits the body of the ideal man into the square and the circle.

Tallest and shortest

The growth of the body is controlled by the pituitary gland in the brain. If it overdoes it, a person will grow into a giant. If it doesn't work, a person will be small. Pygmies grow less than 1.5 m (five feet) tall. The tallest man in the world was American Robert Wadlow. He was 2.7 m (eight feet 11 inches) when he died in 1940.

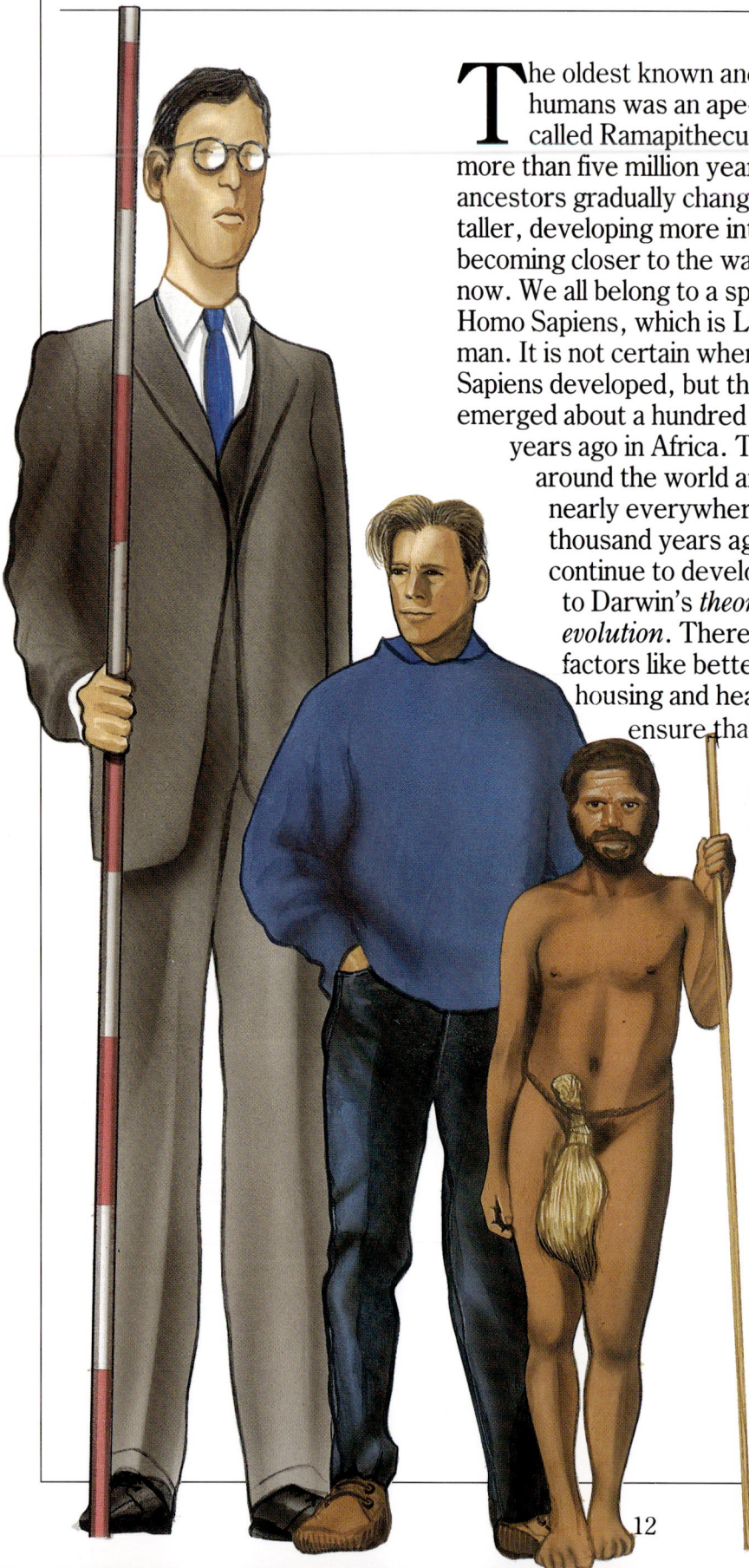

Measuring height

Heights are measured accurately by a *theodolite*, which is a telescope with a scale in it. You can estimate a tree's height by putting someone beside it whose height you know and working out how much taller the tree is.

THE TALLEST LIVING THINGS

The tallest animal is a giraffe which stands 3.5 m (17 feet). The tallest tree was a Douglas fir in Canada which measured 126.5 m (415 feet).

The tallest building

The world's tallest building which is lived in is the Sears Tower in Chicago, USA. It's an office block with 110 floors which rises 443 m (1454 feet). By comparison the Eiffel Tower in Paris which was built in 1889 rises 300 m (990 feet).

How it stays up

Two technical developments were essential before skyscrapers could be built, and both happened in America. Lifts to carry people up all those floors were first made in the 1850's. Then in about 1882 a system was devised to support the walls and floors of buildings on an iron or steel frame. This meant floors could be stacked up like the sections of a bookcase.

How to divide land?

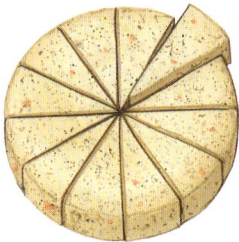

Equal division
Angles are measured in degrees. A cake can be divided equally when you know that a circle is made up of 360 degrees.

Dividers
Dividers like these have been used by sailors for hundreds of years to measure distances on charts.

Geometry is the branch of mathematics concerned with measuring shape. It was first developed in Egypt to define the boundaries of fields, and then in the design of buildings. It made it possible to measure land over large areas and make maps. It also led to the development of astronomy. The invention of instruments using geometry to calculate where you are from the position of the Sun and the stars helped sailors to navigate accurately at sea, when they were out of sight of land.

Ptolemy
The Greek astronomer, Ptolemy, was the first to take a scientific approach to geography. He developed the idea of latitude and longitude hundreds of years before instruments were developed that were reliable enough to measure them.

Latitude and longitude
These are imaginary lines which form a grid on the Earth's surface. Latitude lines run parallel with the equator, north and south. Longitude lines run from pole to pole east and west of the *Greenwich Meridian line*.

Ancient Egypt
The Egyptian groma was an early *surveyor's* instrument. Stones hung from crossed sticks set at right angles to each other helped with marking out distant objects or features.

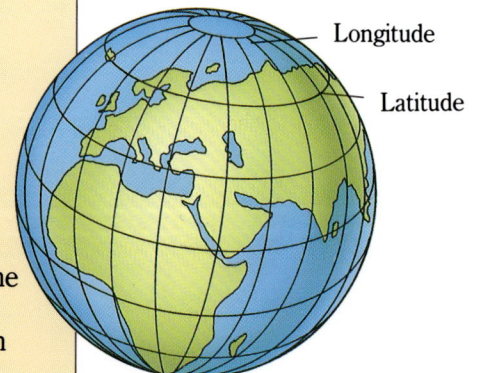

Longitude

Latitude

Euclid

Geometry comes from the Greek words for measuring land. Euclid defined the subject in *Elements of Geometry*, the world's most studied book next to the Bible. It was a school textbook for more than two thousand years.

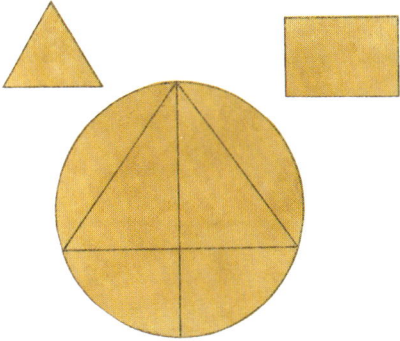

Triangle, square and circle are all geometric shapes.

In this copy of a painting of 1494, an Italian mathematician, Luca Pacioli, is teaching a pupil geometry. The open book is a copy of Euclid's *Elements of Geometry* and there are various geometric shapes in the painting.

Perspective

Perspective conveys the height, breadth and depth of objects, and their relationship to other objects. We are not born with a sense of perspective, we have to learn it. Artists developed perspective during the Italian *Renaissance* in the 15th century as they tried to make their pictures more realistic. These buildings look real.

Vanishing Point

In perspective, parallel railway lines come together in the distance. Where they appear to converge on the horizon is known as the vanishing point. Your mind knows that the lines are still parallel. The narrowing is an indication of distance. Try drawing a railway line going to vanishing point and draw trees along it in perspective.

KETTLETHORPE HIGH SCHOOL

How deep the sea is?

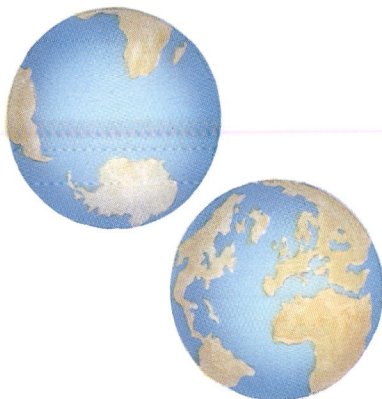

Water covers nearly three quarters of the Earth's surface, but we know little of what goes on under the sea because it is difficult to explore. There are five main oceans, the Pacific, Atlantic, Indian, Southern, and Arctic and water slowly circulates between them in *currents* at different levels. Their average depth is 4,000 m (13,000 ft), but the deepest trench off the Philippines is 11,000 m (36,000 ft) deep. As you descend the *pressure* of water increases, it gets colder and the light fades. On the ocean bed the pressure can be 300 times greater than at the surface which would crush humans and all ships except those specially built to withstand it.

EARLY MEASUREMENT

The risk of running aground in shallow water was a constant anxiety for sailors before the invention of sonar. Measuring depth involved lowering a weighted rope over the side. It was slow and not always accurate as the rope might not go straight to the bottom.

VOYAGE OF THE CHALLENGER

In 1872, Charles Thomson led a round-the-world expedition in HMS *Challenger*. Its aim was to discover new forms of life in the deepest parts of the sea, measure water temperature and chart the main sea currents of the world. When it returned more than three years and 110,000 km (68,000 miles) later, the Royal Society said: 'Never did an expedition cost so little and produce such momentous results for human knowledge.'

Islands occur where undersea peaks break the surface.

The ocean floor

The geography of the sea bed is similar to dry land. Ranges of hills, high mountains, deep valleys, and rolling plains. Much of the ocean floor is covered with sand and silt from rivers. Plants and animals live near the surface. When they die their remains form a sediment on the bottom where the great pressure of the water above turns them into rock. There are also valuable minerals there.

Continental shelf is the terrace at the edge of land, sloping down to 200 metres (600 feet).

EARLY DIVING EQUIPMENT

The first watertight diving suit was invented in 1830 and a variation is still in use. It consisted of a metal helmet with a porthole and a rubber suit connected to the surface by a rope and a breathing line.

Bathyscaphe

A Swiss scientist, Auguste Picard (1884–1962), designed the first bathyscaphe which is a navigable diving vessel built to withstand the enormous pressure at great depths. Similar vessels are used for exploration and salvage, as well as repairing pipelines and oil rigs.

SONAR

Sonar is the system of using sound waves to measure depth or detect underwater objects and submarines. Ships send out pulses of sound. By counting the time it takes for the sound to be reflected back they can work out underwater distances.

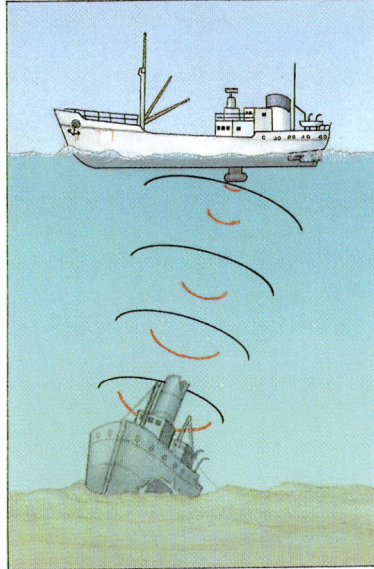

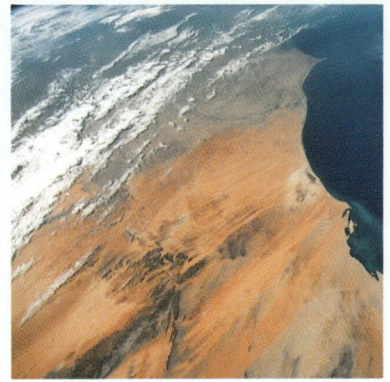

SATELLITE MAPPING

Very accurate maps of the Earth's surface can be made from information gathered by satellites. They can provide the exact positions of coastlines, river estuaries and islands. Computers process the information to work out depths, temperatures and the flow of currents. This can help weather forecasters and fishermen to find fish.

Undersea mountains may be formed by volcanic activity.

The bathyscaphe *Trieste* dived a record 10,916 m (35,810 ft) in the Pacific.

The Marianas Trench off the Philippines could swallow Mount Everest.

If the bath will overflow?

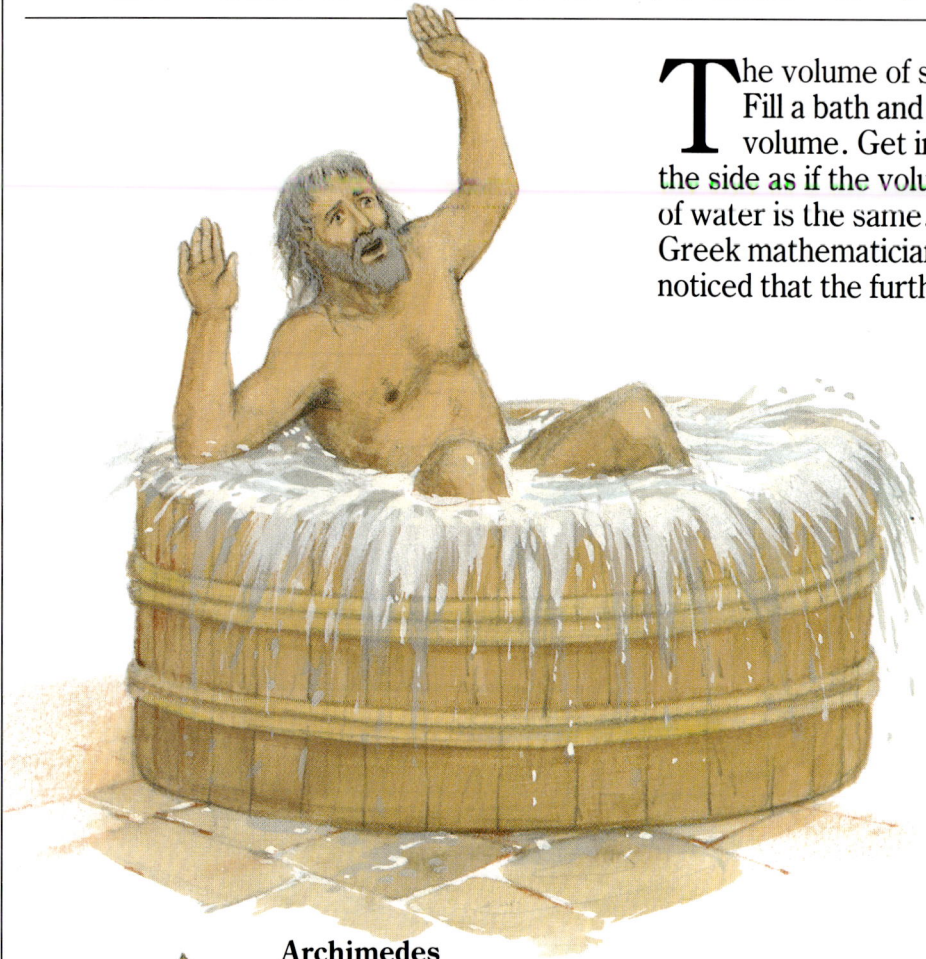

The volume of something is the space it takes up. Fill a bath and the water in it is measured by volume. Get into the bath and the level rises up the side as if the volume has increased, but the amount of water is the same. Something else is happening. A Greek mathematician, Archimedes (287–212 BC), noticed that the further he sank into his bath the more the water rose up. He worked out that his body was displacing an amount of water equal in weight to his body's weight. He jumped out of his bath shouting 'eureka, eureka', which is Greek for 'I've got it.' Another way of measuring volume is by capacity, which is the holding power of something. The capacity of a milk carton is measured by how much liquid it holds. Volume can also be used to measure compact solids like bricks.

Archimedes

Archimedes used his discovery to solve a problem for the King of Syracuse in Sicily. The king suspected he'd been cheated by a goldsmith who had made his crown out of a mixture of gold and cheaper metal, instead of pure gold. But how could he prove it? Archimedes took a block of pure gold weighing the same as the crown and immersed them separately in water. They displaced different volumes of water which meant the crown was larger than the gold block and couldn't be pure gold. The goldsmith was executed!

You can experiment with *displacement* using a half full jar of water. Mark the water level then put in something heavy, like a stone, and see how far the water rises. Try something that floats and measure that.

BUOYANCY

The buoyancy of water, which is its ability to keep objects afloat, increases with the amount of salt in it. You float better in the sea than in a swimming pool. High *evaporation* makes the Dead Sea seven times saltier than normal seas.

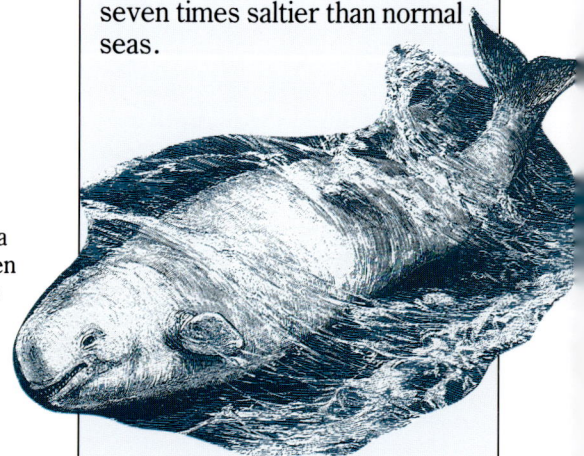

Displacement

A steel ship weighing thousands of tonnes floats, even when loaded with cargo, because it has many empty spaces inside. This means the volume of the ship weighs less than the volume of the water it displaces. If the ship is entirely filled, with, say, water, it will sink.

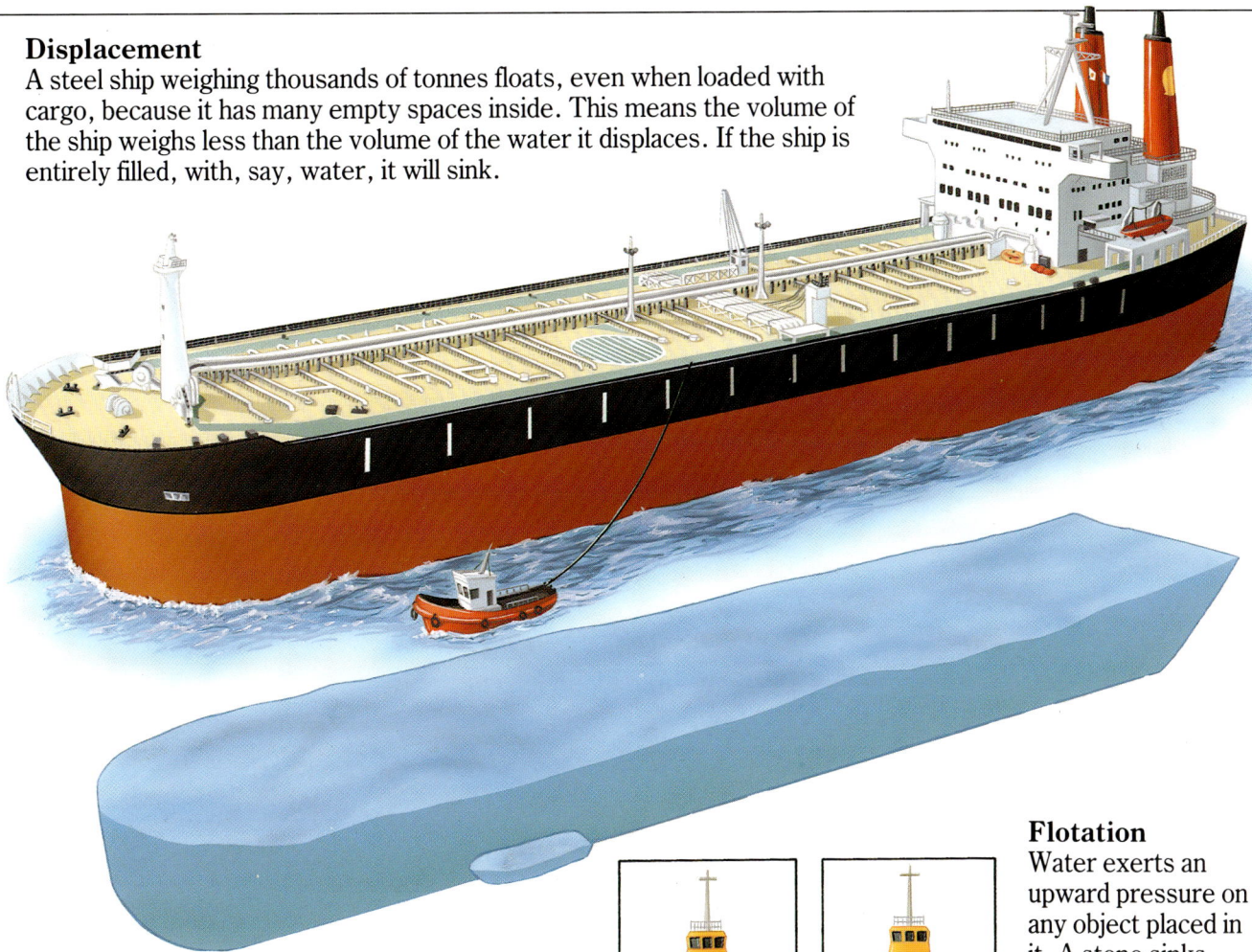

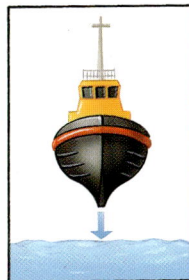

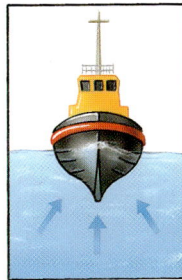

Flotation

Water exerts an upward pressure on any object placed in it. A stone sinks because it's too heavy for the upward pressure, but still weighs less in water than in air.

VOLUME MEASUREMENTS

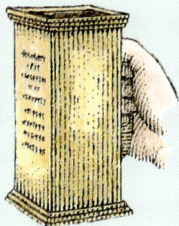

Bronze ale quart
This tankard measuring a quart, or two pints, was used for working out tax on beer.

Gill
A gill is a quarter of a pint. It's use now is mostly limited to measuring spirits.

Fluid ounce
A fluid ounce is the capacity needed to contain an ounce weight of water or other liquids.

Pint
Twenty fluid ounces make one pint. It's one of the few imperial measurements continuing after full *metrication*.

Gallon
Eight pints make a gallon. Although a liquid measure, it was first defined as the volume of eight pounds of wheat.

Water in bath
A standard size bath, when filled to the overflow, holds between forty and forty-five gallons (150–200 litres) of water.

The Litre
A litre is the volume in a cube whose edge is one tenth of a metre. It's equal to 1.76 pints. The volume of 1 kg of water is one litre.

How big a city is?

About a third of the world's population lives in cities, which continually grow and change. Wherever they are, cities tend to share common features. The centre has the local government, and sometimes the national government, buildings. There is a business area and a shopping area. Around these are the inner housing areas. Factories are usually on the outskirts, and beyond them are the suburbs where most people live. Some are planned from the beginning and others, like London, developed naturally as villages grew into each other. An important city can be called a metropolis. In some countries cities are growing into each other. A supercity like this is called a megalopolis.

Acres and hectares
Acre is a unit of land measurement. The metric unit is the hectare which is about two and a half times larger. An acre was traditionally the amount of land a team of oxen could plough in a day.

Growth of a city
1. A prehistoric settlement was the first stage in the growth of many modern cities. For it to grow there had to be enough surplus food to feed non-agricultural workers who could build. A river or coast location helped trade and communications.
2. The Greeks created city states, but as cities grew they encountered technical problems of water supply, sewage and administration. The Romans solved many of these.
3. The Industrial Revolution led to the rapid expansion of cities as people left the countryside to find work in them. The crowding this caused eased when public transport allowed people to live in outer suburbs.

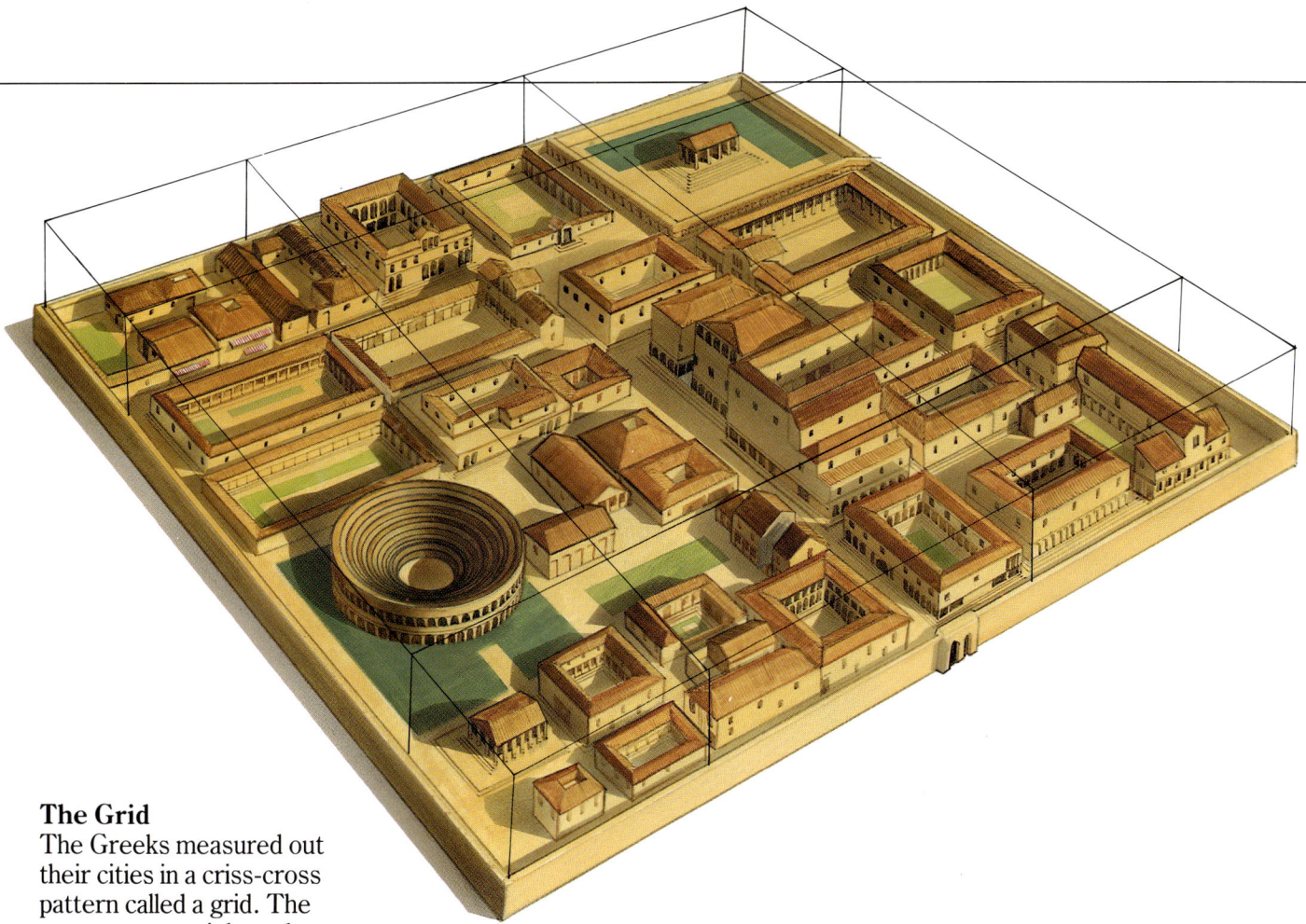

The Grid
The Greeks measured out their cities in a criss-cross pattern called a grid. The streets are straight and they run at right angles to each other. The Romans adopted this pattern after they conquered Greece.

The modern city
Planned cities are much more common in recently developed countries with the space to lay them out. When European settlers arrived in Australia a little over 200 years ago they found a vast country sparsely inhabited by Aborigines and without buildings. Melbourne is laid out on a grid beside the Yarra River.

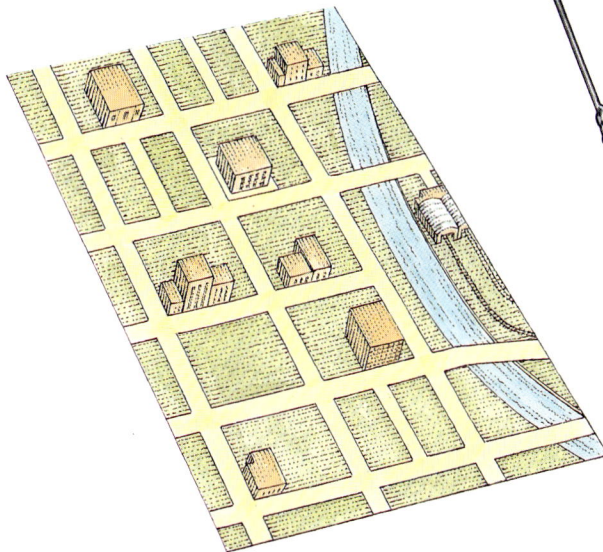

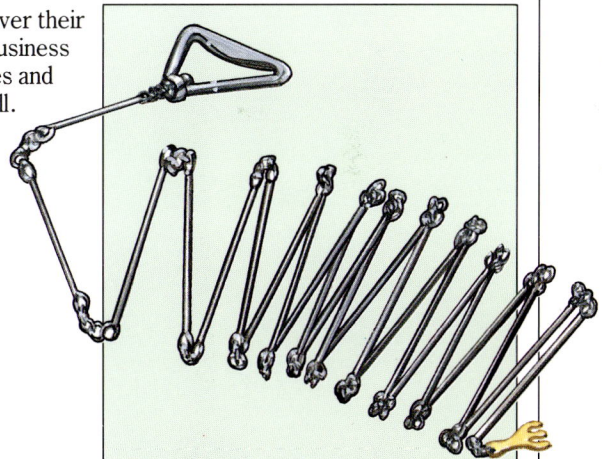

Roman city
The Romans laid out the towns they built all over their empire to a similar plan. The forum was the business centre, there were housing areas, bath-houses and temples. Most towns were protected by a wall.

MEASURING AREA
The Egyptians measured land with a long rope, knotted at intervals of a cubit, about 45.7 cms (21 inches). This became a chain of a hundred links totalling 20.1 m (22 yards) with a handle and markers. The links gave a chain flexibility and reliability, and they have been used to measure distances of hundreds of kilometres as well as small areas like gardens.

How heavy we are?

Gravity is the force which pulls everything towards Earth. The effect of this force is called weight. If you weighed yourself on top of a mountain you would be about 225 gm (half a pound) lighter than at sea level because you would be further away from the centre of the Earth. The pound in weight comes from the Roman pound which was called libra. This is why the symbol for pound is lb. When gold coins were in everyday use they were worth exactly what they weighed and could be checked. Reliable weights were needed for trade, and early traders used natural things which didn't vary much. A grain of wheat became a 'grain' of weight, which is used for medicines, and the carob seed became the 'carat' for weighing precious stones.

By hand
The first scales were human. People balanced a handful of, say, nuts against a handful of vegetables to see which weighed more.

Roman scales
Coins were placed in one pan of this Roman beam balance and known weights were put in the other. A pointer at the beam's centre showed when the pans balanced.

The balance of life
The balance is the first known scientific instrument, and it was invented at least 7000 years ago. In Egypt it was also used in religious ceremonies. Here, a dead man's heart in a jar is put into one pan of the scales and the god of truth and justice sits in the other.

THE METRIC SYSTEM
Antoine Lavoisier (1743–1794) is called the father of modern chemistry for his work classifying chemicals. He carried out many of the experiments to decide the weight of the kilogram in the new metric system. It was decided that a kilogram should be the weight of a thousand cubic centimetres of water.

The Kilogram
After a while scientists decided that water was an unreliable yardstick. For one thing, its weight varies with temperature and *density*. A master kilogram weight, made of platinum and iridium, is kept under three glass domes at the International Bureau of Weights near Paris. Exact copies are distributed throughout the world.

Bathroom scales

The weight on the platform of scales is transmitted thorugh a system of *levers* to a pointer. This moves along a scale of weights until it reaches your weight. Electronic scales use integrated circuits like computers.

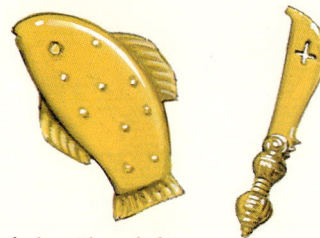

Ashanti weights
The Ashanti come from a gold mining region of Africa where Ghana is now. In the eighteenth century they made ornamental weights from gold, often in the shape of animals and fish.

The stone
The stone weight was . . . a stone. The problem was it was impossible to find stones everywhere which weighed the same. It was eventually standardised at 14 pounds and used for weighing people.

Elizabeth I
Elizabeth I (1533–1603) reformed the system of weights after a six year investigation. All existing weights were destroyed and new ones introduced in 1588 which remained standard for 250 years.

Baker's Dozen
Bread loses weight as it loses moisture. For centuries bakers had to supply thirteen loaves to the dozen in case any of them was under the standard baker's dozen weight.

HEAVIEST PERSON EVER
The world's heaviest man was Walter Hudson of New York. He weighed 540 kg (85 stone or 1190 pounds), which is more than half a ton. when he died in 1992 his coffin had to be reinforced with steel.

Hundredweight
Sometimes things went wrong. For some reason Edward I (1239–1307) decided the hundredweight should be 112 pounds instead of 100!

Santorio Santorio
The Italian doctor, Santorio Santorio (1561–1636), built a weighing chair to study the effect on his body's weight of eating, excreting and even sleeping. He spent most of thirty years of his life in the chair, despite being the professor of medicine at Padua University. Among other things he discovered that the body can lose weight by sweating.

How solid metal is?

Take a ten-pin bowling ball and a cannonball. They're about the same size and they're both solid. You can pick one up easily and bowl it but you can hardly move the other. They weigh different amounts, but why? The molecules in the iron of the cannonball are crowded together much more tightly than the molecules of the wood in the bowling ball. The cannonball is denser. Density is measured in grams per cubic centimetre (pounds per square inch). To find the density of the cannonball its volume and *mass* are compared.

Different densities
All these objects have different densities. The material in each is packed together more, or less, densely than in the others.

Density and volume
Even different metals have different densities. Density can be measured by putting something in water and seeing how much water it displaces (see pages 16–17). Gold is much denser than aluminium. A block of gold weighing the same as a block of aluminium will be smaller because it is denser.

Galileo's hydrostatic balance
Galileo did experiments with a balance to discover the pressure exerted by water. An object weighs less in water than out of it because of water pressure.

An aeroplane has great weight and mass. To overcome the force of gravity and fly, it has hugely powerful engines and a specially designed shape.

SUBMARINES
A submarine has hollow ballast tanks on the outside of its hull. When these are filled with air the submarine floats. When they are filled with water the submarine dives. It manoeuvres underwater using fins called hydroplanes. To surface again water is blown out of the tanks with compressed air. The first nuclear submarine was built in the United States in 1954.

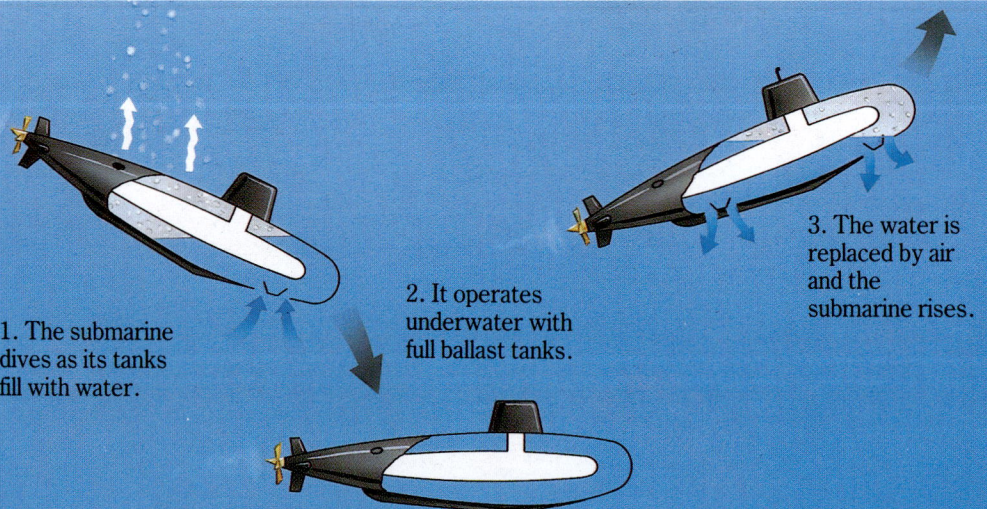

1. The submarine dives as its tanks fill with water.

2. It operates underwater with full ballast tanks.

3. The water is replaced by air and the submarine rises.

Mass and gravity

The distinction between weight and mass is best demonstrated by an astronaut. Before he leaves Earth the astronaut has mass, which is the amount of matter in his body, and weight because weight is the effect of gravity pulling on that mass. Once in space he is beyond reach of the Earth's gravity and becomes weightless. But his mass remains the same wherever he is, he still has the same amount of matter in his body as he had on Earth. If he bumps into another astronaut he'll still hurt himself and come up in a bruise. Back on Earth the more mass something has the more it resists being speeded up or slowed down. A truck is harder to stop than a car travelling at the same speed.

1. On Earth an astronaut has mass and weight.

2. In space the astronaut is weightless but still full of mass.

PLIMSOLL LINE

Plimsoll lines are painted on ships' hulls and it is illegal to overload them so that the line is below water. This mark shows the people who load the ship when they must stop adding cargo. If they overload the ship it will sink.

Samuel Plimsoll's idea saved many sailors' lives.

Icebergs

When water freezes it expands. Icebergs float because their volume is very slightly more than the weight of water they displace. Ninety per cent of an iceberg is submerged. The largest iceberg, seen in the Pacific in 1956, was the size of Belgium.

How much energy it takes to light a bulb?

Electricity is one of the universal forces of nature. It exists everywhere, but its effects are only noticeable when it moves, or flows. Electricity is created by power stations and batteries. It provides energy. This energy can be weak, like the electric shocks we sometimes get from touching metal, or very strong, like a lightning bolt. Electricity is measured in watts, volts and amperes. Energy is measured in joules. Power is the rate at which energy is changed. One watt means one joule of energy is being changed every second. A 100 watt light bulb is changing 100 joules of electrical energy into the same amount of heat energy each second.

STATIC ELECTRICITY

An electrical charge which builds up and is unable to flow is called static electricity. Create one by rubbing a balloon against yourself and then sticking it to a wall.

Lightning strikes

Benjamin Franklin (1706–1790) was an American statesman and scientist with a keen interest in electricity. In 1752 he flew a kite in a storm with a key dangling from the wet string. The sparks which came off the key proved his theory that lightning was itself a huge electrical spark. Luckily, he also invented the lightning conductor which protects tall buildings by attracting lightning and channelling it harmlessly to Earth. A lightning flash contains 100 million volts, and can kill or seriously burn anyone it strikes.

The measurers of electricity

Luigi Galvani (1737–1798) was a professor of anatomy at Bologna University where he noticed twitching in the muscles of frogs' legs during an experiment. He decided that these must be caused by electricity.

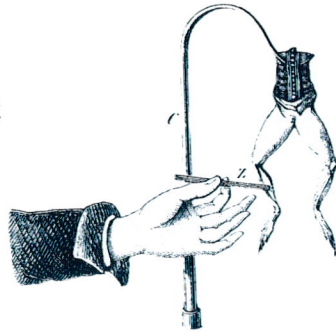

Alessandro Volta (1745–1827) discovered that the twitching was not caused by 'animal' electricity as some people thought, but by the contact of two different metals which produced electricity and made the muscles twitch. He gave his name to the volt, the unit of electric potential, or force.

James Watt (1736–1819) was the Scottish engineer who made steam engines efficient. A watt is the unit of energy used in a second.

Thomas Edison (1847–1931) was the American inventor of electric light. A wire inside a glass bulb from which the air had been removed glows white hot when electricity passed through it.

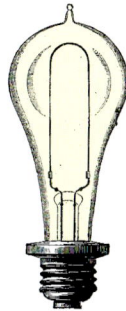

The power of a bulb is measured in watts.

Batteries

Large batteries are divided into cells and use chemicals to store electricity. They can also be charged up with electricity from outside to last a long time.

The chemicals that make electricity in small batteries are quickly used up.

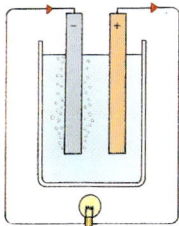

Currents

Flowing electrons make a current. Current is measured in amperes, named after André Ampère (1775–1836), a French scientist who made important discoveries about electricity and magnetism.

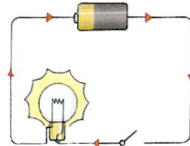

A circuit is the circular path along which electricity flows from one terminal of a battery or generator to the other.

It is important for people working with electricity to know how much is being supplied along the circuit, the current, and how much force it has, the voltage. An ammeter works by changing some of the electricity into magnetism which moves a needle on a dial. The electrician can read off the strength of the current and the voltage.

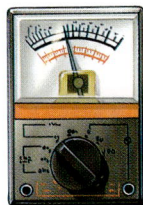

ENERGY IN THE HOME

The electricity we use at home is generated in power stations by turbines which are made to spin rapidly by steam. For efficient transmission voltage is stepped up by *transformers* to 400,000 volts. It is stepped down again before it enters a factory (33,000 volts) or your home (240 volts).

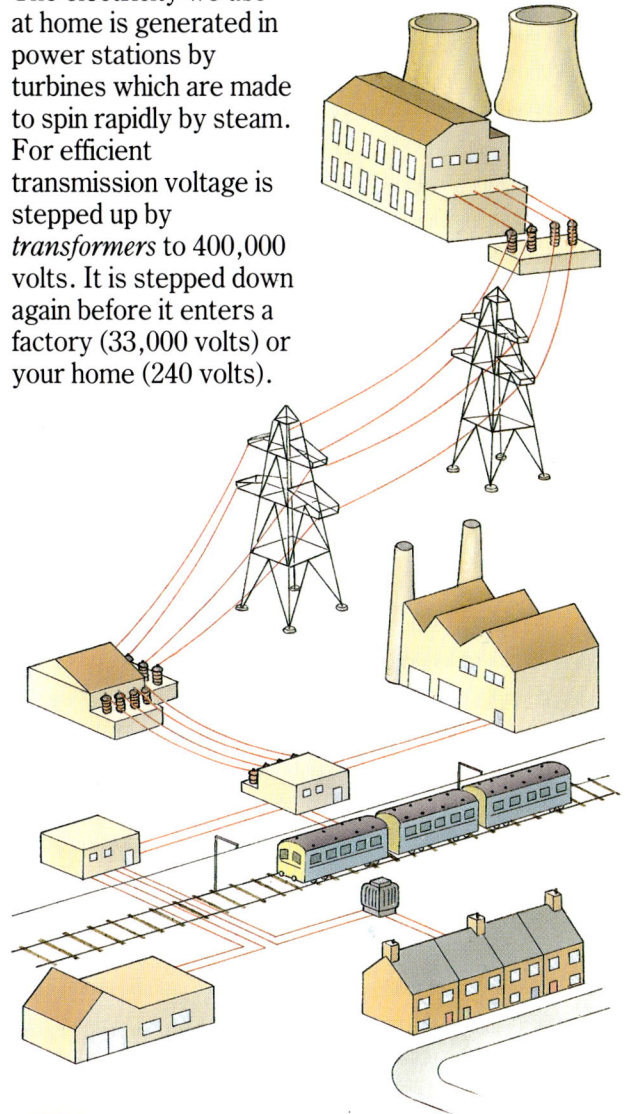

Forms of energy

The steam in most power stations is heated by burning coal, oil or gas, or by nuclear reaction. The first three will run out one day, and burning them produces pollution. Nuclear energy produces no atmospheric pollutants but poisonous *radioactive* waste. Other, cleaner forms of energy are solar power from the Sun, windmills, *hydroelectric* power from moving water, tidal power from the rise and fall of the sea and *geothermal* power from hot rocks underground.

There's energy in food?

Food provides the energy your body needs to move around, grow and stay healthy. There are three sources of energy, or nourishment. Protein, which is what your body is mostly built of, carbohydrates, which include sugars and starches that are rapidly turned into energy, and fats which are a good source of heat. The body stores fats under the skin. There are also vitamins and minerals which are important in small amounts to keep you healthy. Food contains things the body can't use. Fibre helps the body get rid of waste material.

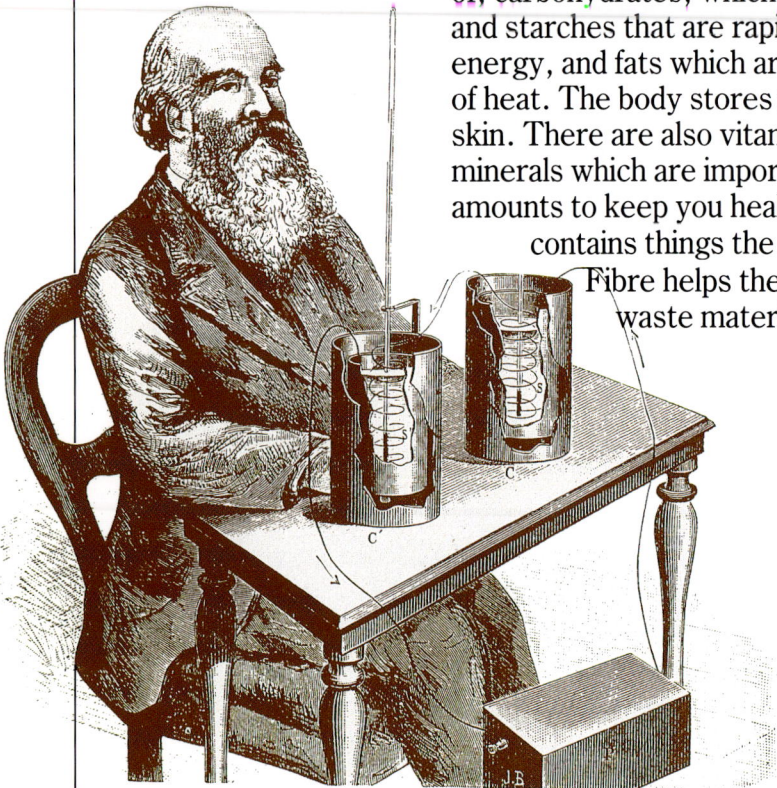

JOULES AND CALORIES
The joule is the basic unit of energy. There are 4.2 joules to the calorie which is the unit of heat. One calorie is the amount of heat needed to raise the temperature of one gram of water by one degree celsius.

Food is converted into heat to measure energy.

James Joule
James Joule (1818–1889) was an amateur scientist who was fascinated by heat. He explained that energy is never used up, it changes into different forms. This became known as the law of the conservation of energy.

Calculating food energy
A bomb calorimeter calculates food energy. Food placed in the metal container, called the bomb, is electrically ignited, and it heats water as it burns. The rise in temperature can be converted into joules or calories.

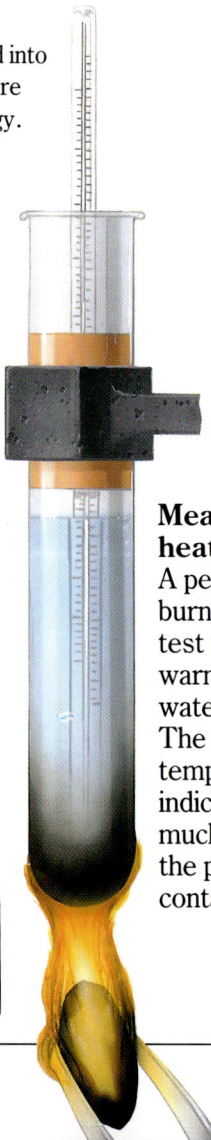

Measuring by heat
A peanut burned under a test tube will warm up the water inside. The rise in temperature indicates how much energy the peanut contained.

Food chains

1. The Sun is the source of all energy in the world and where the food chain starts.

2. Plants use sunlight to convert water and carbon dioxide from the air into food. This is *photosynthesis*.

3. Herbivores such as cows and sheep get their energy from eating the green plants.

4. At the end of the food chain are animals that eat meat and plants, called omnivores.

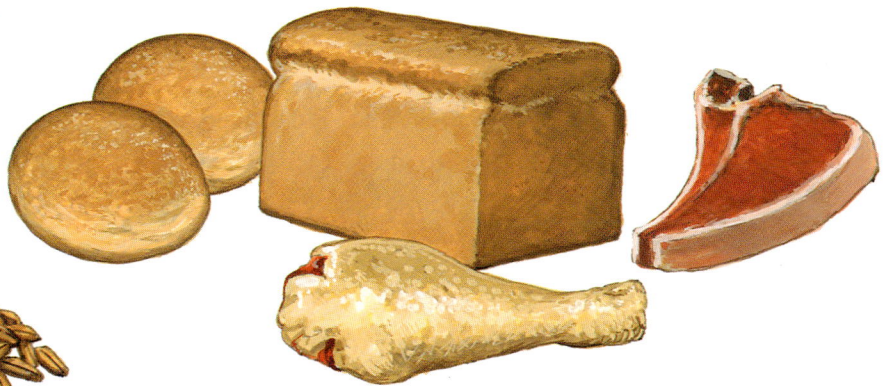

Fruit contains some protein and carbohydrate and a lot of water. Fruit contains a lot of vitamin C. It is low in calories (24–70 calories per 100 grams).

Vegetables contain some carbohydrate and protein, a little fat, water and vitamins. High in fibre and low in calories (10–80 calories per 100 grams).

Grains are mainly carbohydrates and include rice, wheat and sweetcorn. They contain a lot of fibre and are high in calories (240–380 calories per 100 grams).

Meat is nearly all protein with a lot of fat. Rich in vitamins and minerals, and high in calories (150–300 calories per 100 grams).

HOW MUCH ENERGY DO WE NEED IN A DAY?

Children of eight need 2000 calories, (88000 kilojoules).

Teenagers need between 2300 and 3000 calories (9600 kj – 12600 kj)

Men doing office work need 2750 calories (11550 kj), women 2250 (9450 kj).

Athletes need between 3000 (12600 kg) for women and 3500 (1500 kj) for men.

How fast a car goes?

The first cars with petrol engines were made in the 1880's in Germany. Early cars were hand built, expensive and slow. Cars in Britain had to have someone walking in front with a red warning flag. Henry Ford installed a production line in his factories in 1907 to mass produce the cheap and reliable Model T Ford. Over the years cars have become faster and more reliable as they have developed. The speed of a car or any object travelling is measured by how much distance it covers in what time. So measurements can be in kilometres per hour or miles per hour, or other units of distance and time, like metres per second.

Fastest Recorded Speeds

One horse power, enough to carry a rider or pull a cart.

Three horse power for a war chariot.

HORSE POWER

When machines were first used in factories they replaced horses. Engineers measured the power of the machines by comparing them to horses. One horsepower is the energy needed to lift 250 kg (550 lbs) 30 cms (one foot) in a second. A two horsepower engine delivers twice the energy.

A family saloon has between 60 and 100 horsepower.

An electric locomotive has about 5000 horsepower.

A 25,000 ton cargo ship has about 16,000 horsepower.

This early car was powered by steam, built by Nicholas Cugnot in France in 1769.

1890 Panhard Levasior. The first car to have the engine in the front.

The fastest boat is *The Texan* driven by Eddie Hill, USA, which reached 368.5 kph (229 mph) in California in 1982.

The fastest person is Carl Lewis, USA, who ran 100 m in 9.86 seconds in the 1991 World Athletics Championships in Tokyo.

The fastest motorbike is *Lightning Bolt*, ridden by Donald Vesco, USA, which reached 512 kph (318 mph) in Utah in 1978.

VELOCITY

Velocity is the speed of an object travelling in a particular direction. Uniform velocity requires the object to travel in a straight line at a steady speed. This hardly ever happens with a car. It is how bullets and rockets are measured.

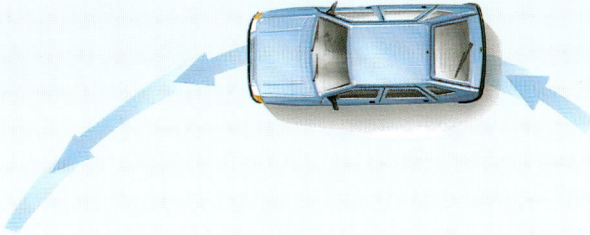

Speed

Speed is the rate at which distance is covered. A car travelling in a circle at 80 kph (50 mph) has a uniform speed but not velocity because its direction is constantly changing.

Streamlining for speed

Wind tunnel testing, first used for planes, is now an important part of the design stage of new cars. Hundreds of changes may be made to the body profile to streamline the car. Designers are trying to reduce drag, the *air resistance* on a moving object which slows it down. Smoke streamers in the wind tunnel show air movement over the car.

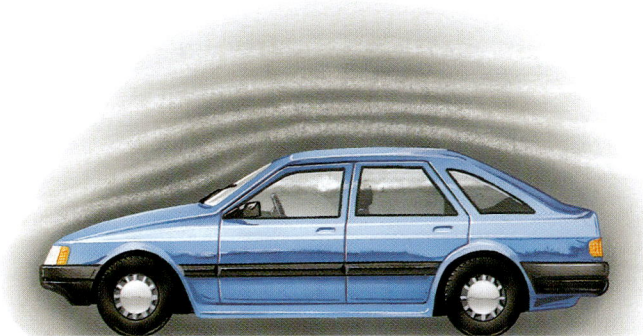

Speed of light

If you travelled at the speed of light you could circle the Earth more than seven times in a second.

The fastest car is *Thrust 2*, powered by two jet engines, which covered a mile in Nevada in 1983 at 1015 kph (633 mph).

The fastest aircraft is the American spyplane, *Blackbird*, which covered a 25 mile course in California at 3525 kph (2193 mph) in 1976.

ERNST MACH

Aerodynamics is the science of flight and it is increasingly used in the development of cars. The Austrian physicist, Ernst Mach (1838–1916), discovered many of the important principles in wave dynamics. He photographed the *shock waves* of objects travelling at high speed and set out new, more scientific methods for observing and measuring such movement. He gave his name to Mach numbers, used in aerodynamics. The velocity of a plane is divided by the velocity of sound, so that a plane flying at the speed of sound is flying at Mach 1, at twice the speed of sound, Mach 2, and so on.

The Time?

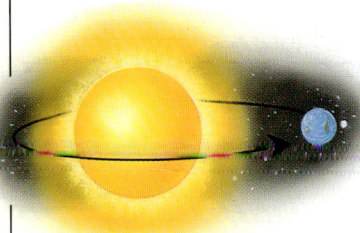

A complete circuit
A year is the time it takes for the Earth to make a complete circuit round the Sun. The Egyptians first measured it by comparing the Sun's movement with the River Nile's flooding.

It became important to know the time when people first became farmers. It was good enough to have just an approximate idea, and the methods used were not very accurate. The shadows cast by the Sun as it moved was the first way of keeping track of the passing day. The time it took for a candle to burn, or water to flow, were others. The first mechanical clocks were introduced in the thirteenth century in Europe. Their workings gradually became more reliable and accurate as well as small enough to put into watches. Now, time seems to be in control of, indeed rule, everything we do.

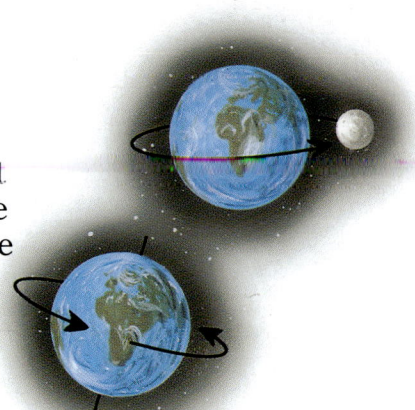

Months and days
Months were measured by the Moon. From one new Moon to the next is 29½ days. A day is the time it takes for the Earth to make a complete turn on its own *axis*.

Time zones
An international agreement was reached in 1884 to set time round the world according to the time at the Royal observatory at Greenwich near London, Greenwich Mean Time (GMT). The world was divided into 24 time zones, each of an hour. Places within a zone use the same time.

As you travel west you put your watch back an hour for every zone crossed.

As you travel east you put your watch forward an hour for every zone crossed.

The International Date Line is opposite to the Greenwich Meridian and marks where one day ends and the next begins.

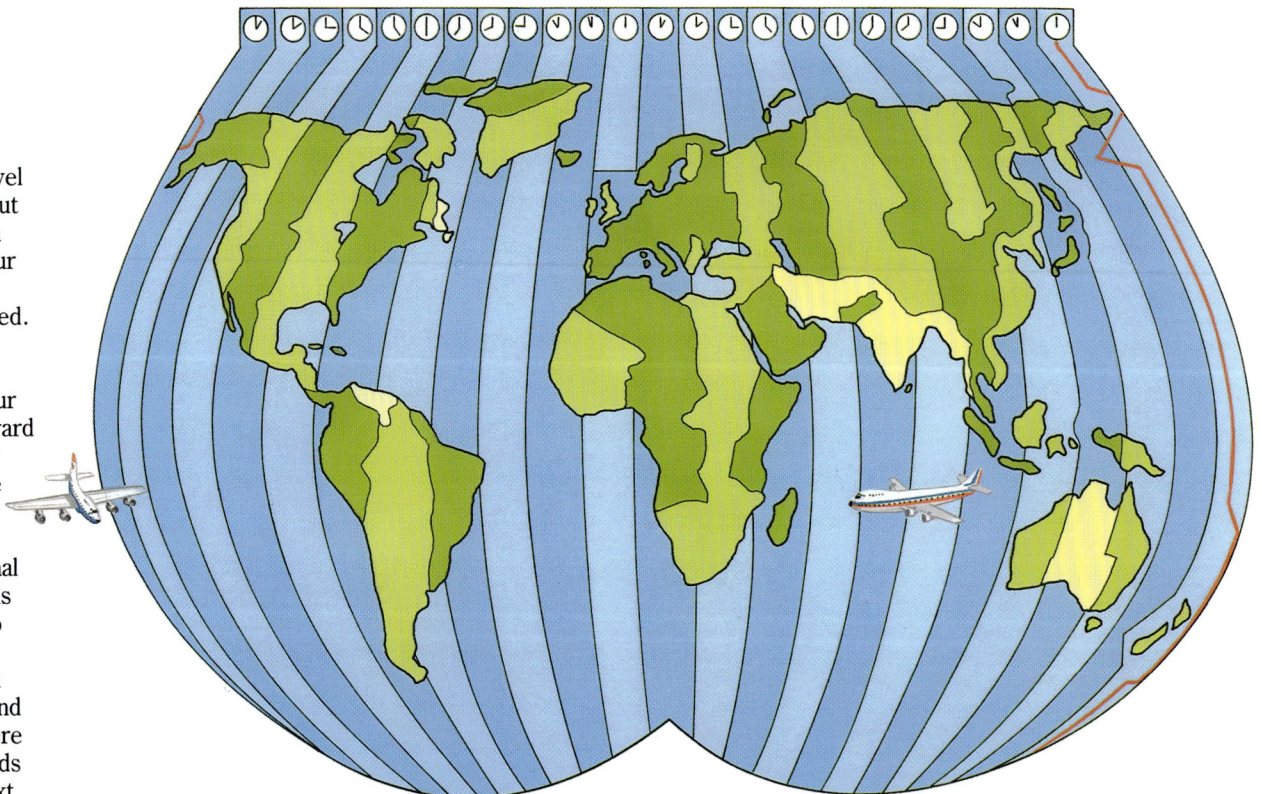

Sundials

Sundials were one of the earliest ways of measuring time. They're mentioned in the Old Testament of the Bible. The Sun's shadow moves round a dial divided into hours. But its no good at night or on a cloudy day.

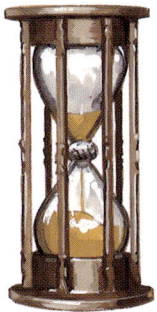

Hourglass

Accuracy improved with the development of the hourglass in the Middle Ages. Sand flowed through a narrow gap from one chamber to the other in a fixed time.

Water clock

Water clocks were widely used thousands of years ago in China, Arabia and Europe. Water flows at a set rate out of pots marked with a scale.

GALILEO AND THE PENDULUM

While still a medical student, Galileo (1564–1642) watched a lamp swinging from the ceiling of Pisa cathedral. He timed it using his pulse and discovered the lamp always took the same time to complete a swing from one side to the other. He realised that a pendulum could be used to measure time.

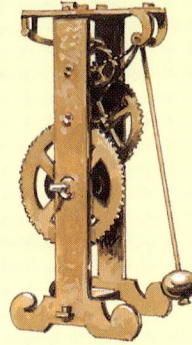

Galileo's pendulum device for measuring time.

Grandfather clock

A grandfather clock's 1 metre (three foot) pendulum takes a second to make a full swing. Altering it's length changes the clock's speed.

Quartz crystals regulate a watch's speed.

Watch case and strap.

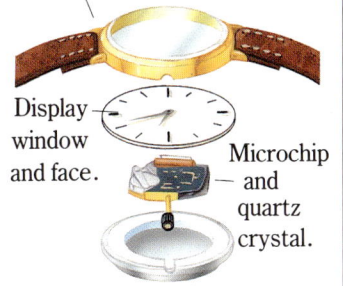

Display window and face.

Microchip and quartz crystal.

Battery and back cover.

Quartz wristwatch

Electricity from the battery makes the quartz vibrate thousands of times a second. The microchip uses the vibrations to change the displayed time every second.

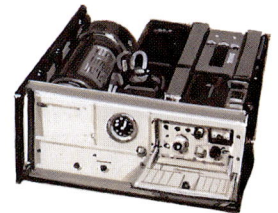

Atomic clock

An atomic clock is the ultimate in accuracy. The clock is tuned to vibrations within atoms of caesium which have an unvarying *frequency*. If it ran for a million years it would be right to within a second.

The White Rabbit in the book *Alice in Wonderland* symbolises our obsession with time. It's always talking about being late.

What The Day Is?

Seasons
The seasons change because the axis, or tilt, of the Earth towards the Sun changes during its annual orbit. The change is barely noticeable at the equator.

Between the rotation of the Earth which marks a day and its *orbit* of the Sun which marks a year there is a lot of time. A calendar is a way of keeping track of this time and arranging it so that people can organise and plan their lives. The Sumerians divided the year into days 4,500 years ago. The Egyptians borrowed that idea when they made the first calendars based on the Sun's movement. They divided the year into twelve months, in three seasons, Flood-time, Seed-time and Harvest-time.

Ancient Hebrew calendar
This calendar was based on the date of the world's creation as given in Jewish scriptures.

Julius Caesar devised the Julian calendar.

The Roman calendar
The calendar we use is based on a Roman one devised by Julius Ceasar more than two thousand years ago. He decided the number of days should be 365 and a quarter

to match the solar year. The names of the months have Latin origins, for example, July after Julius Caesar, August after the Emperor Augustus and March after the god Mars. Errors began to creep into the calendar because later Roman leaders interfered with it and accurate corrections were not made for the extra quarter of a day in the solar year. In 1582 Pope Gregory acted because Church festivals were getting later and later each year. Before the Gregorian Calendar came into effect eleven days had to be 'lost', which caused riots because people thought their lives were being shortened. Pope Gregory decided that century years should not be leap years unless they could be divided by 400.

Pope Gregory corrected the calendar.

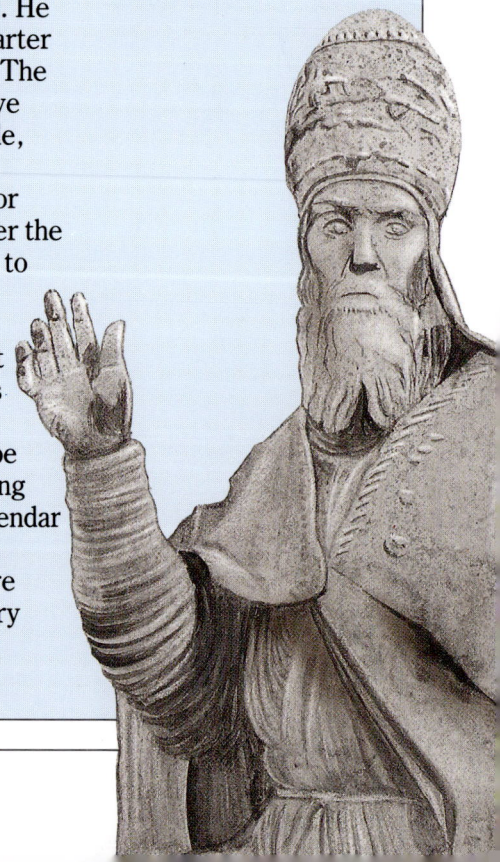

MEASURING THE STARS

The Mayan civilisation flourished in Central America south of the Aztec empire. The Mayans used a calendar of eighteen months divided into twenty days, with a nineteenth month of five nameless days which were considered unlucky. Each of the other days had four ways of identifying it. There was a name and a number for each day in the yearly cycle. There was also a name and a number for each day according to the month.

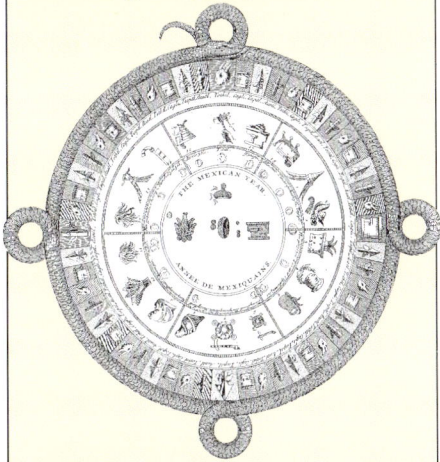

Aztec sunstone

The Aztec Sunstone is a twenty tonne slab of stone carved in the sixteenth century with symbols representing time and history. The face in the middle represents the Sun. The four rectangles round it are four ages when the universe was created and destroyed. Other symbols represent days, months and years.

How hot it is?

The temperature at the centre of the Sun is about 16 million °C (27 million °F). The surface is 6,000 °C.

The centre of the Earth is about 4,500 °C (8,000 °F)

Water boils at 100 °C (212 °F).

Body temperature in humans is 37 °C (98.6 °F).

The freezing point of water is 0 °C (32 °F)

Absolute zero, −273 °C (−450 °F), is the lowest possible temperature.

The Sun doesn't simply give us heat and light. Its energy keeps the atmosphere in continuous motion and that produces wind, rain, clouds, thunder and snow – our weather.

Temperature is a measure of how hot something is. A thermometer is a way of measuring it. Your body has an automatic temperature control. If you get too cold you shiver to produce heat from muscular activity. Too hot and you sweat, and the evaporation of the sweat cools your skin.

Hottest place on Earth
The hottest place on Earth is Death Valley in California. The air temperature can reach 49° Celsius (120° Fahrenheit) in the summer when the ground temperature is near boiling point.

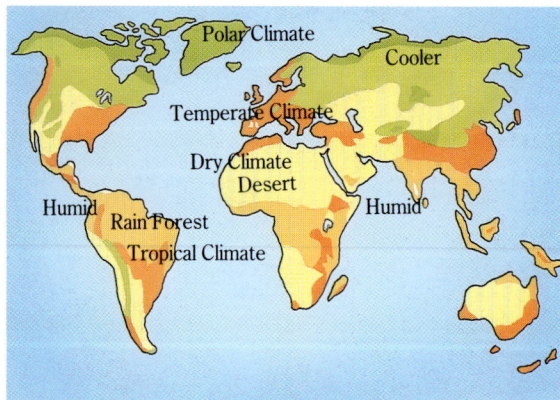

World climate
Climate is the average weather of a particular place. The Greeks divided the world into three broad climatic zones. The Frigid Zones extending from the North and South Poles. The Temperate Zones between these and the Tropics of Cancer and Capricorn. And the Torrid Zone between the Tropics. There are many variations within these zones caused by temperature, rainfall, altitude, wind, cloud and sunshine. Rain forests grow in the Tropics where there is heavy rainfall. The temperate zone has warm summers and cool winters. The climate of an area determines what crops grow there.

The Sun
Because the Earth's surface is curved, the temperature at any particular place mostly depends on its closeness to the Sun.

GLOBAL WARMING
Global warming is caused by gases collecting in the atmosphere. They prevent some of the Sun's heat from being released back into space.

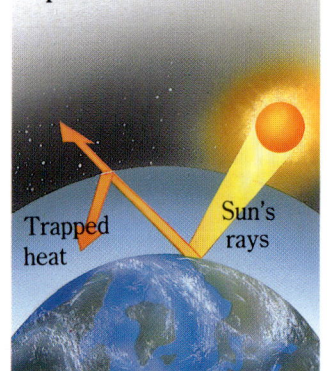

Coldest place on Earth
The coldest place on Earth is the Antarctic with a winter temperature of −58°C (−72°F).

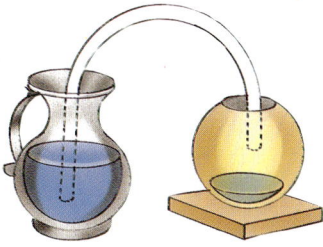

Philo of Byzantium

More than 2,000 years ago Philo of Byzantium connected a container of air to another of water and placed them in the Sun to prove that air expands when heated.

Galileo and a thermometer

Galileo invented the first thermometer in about 1593, called a thermoscope. The air in the bulb expanded or contracted with temperature and made water move up and down the tube.

The Barometer

Evangelista Torricelli (1608–1647) invented the first *barometer* in an experiment in 1644 to create a *vacuum*. He filled a metre (3 ft) tube with mercury. The open end was immersed in a bowl of mercury. The mercury in the tube dropped about 20 cms (4 ins) creating a vacuum in the enclosed end. Torricelli believed atmospheric pressure on the mercury in the bowl stopped the mercury in the tube dropping further.

CELSIUS

Anders Celsius (1701–1744) was the first person to devise a centigrade scale running from 0 to 100. But his 0 was boiling water and the 100 was the melting point of ice. It was reversed after he died. Celsius has come into general use because it's simple and in step with the metric system.

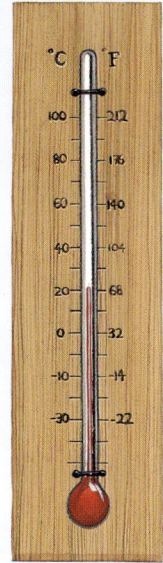

Fahrenheit

Temperature scales for the first thermometers differed greatly. The German scientist, Daniel Fahrenheit (1686–1736), took as the zero for his scale the lowest temperature he knew, the point at which a mixture of ice and salt would freeze. On this scale ordinary ice melts at 32° and water boils at 212°. His scale is still widely used in English speaking countries. Another scale developed by Lord Kelvin starts at absolute zero, −273°C.

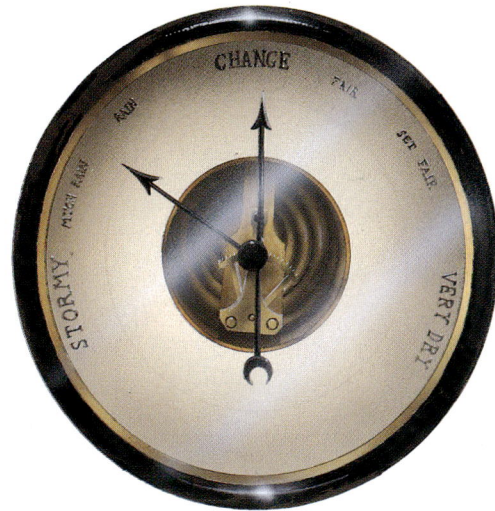

Atmospheric pressure

The weight of the air on the Earth's surface is called the atmospheric pressure. Variations in the pressure take place as the weather changes. In a barometer there is a metal box with a vacuum inside. The top of the box rises or falls as the pressure changes. Levers convert this movement into the movement of a needle on the face of the barometer. A barograph works in a similar way, but uses a pen and a rotating drum of paper to record pressure changes.

How loud an aeroplane is?

All sounds are made by objects vibrating, and anything that vibrates makes a sound. You can see this if you stretch a rubber band and pluck it. Stop it moving and the twanging stops. Sound needs a *medium* to travel through. There is no sound in the vacuum of space. When the rubber band vibrates it pushes against *molecules* of air which in turn push against the molecules next to them, and so sound spreads. It travels faster through solids and liquids because the molecules in them are closer together. The ear funnels sounds to the eardrum. The vibrations pass to tiny hairs attached to nerves which send messages to the brain.

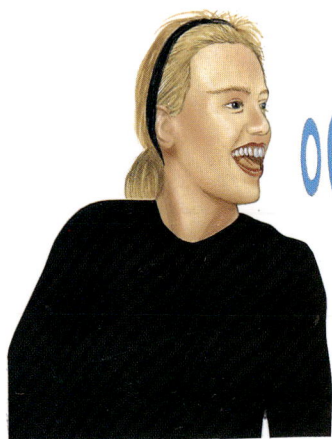

Sound waves
Sound moves in waves, and it travels through air at 1180 kph (740 mph). It travels much faster in water and the sound of a whale can be heard over hundreds of kilometres (miles) of sea. To see how sound travels drop a pebble into a puddle and watch the widening ripples. Sound waves move in a similar way.

MEASURING SOUND

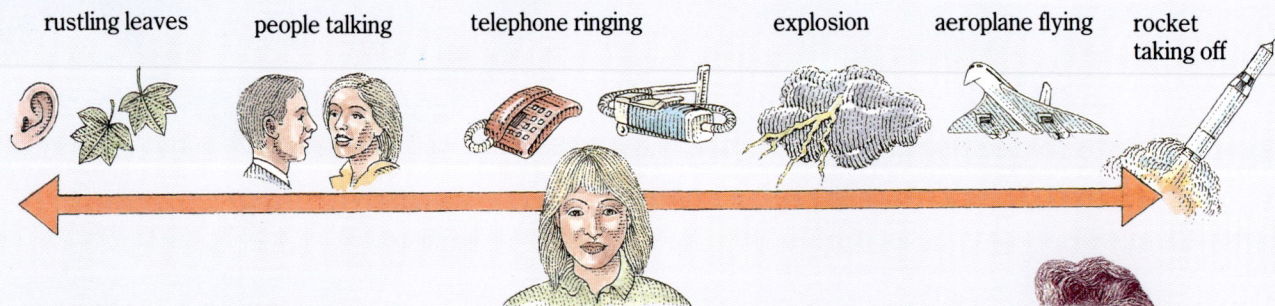

rustling leaves   people talking   telephone ringing   explosion   aeroplane flying   rocket taking off

The loudness of sound was first measured in Bels, after Alexander Bell. But the unit was too large and was replaced by one a tenth of the size, the decibel. The quietest sound the human ear can hear is 0 decibels and the level at which hearing is damaged is 140 decibels. This is called the threshold of pain.

But sounds of a lower level can damage your hearing if they are continuous.

Alexander Bell
Alexander Bell (1847–1922) taught deaf people to speak, and this work led him to invent the telephone in 1876.

Sound barrier

Because sound travels at 1180 kph (740 mph), the sound waves of a plane flying slower than this move ahead of it. As the plane reaches the speed of sound, the sound waves can't get away. They squash up in front of it and create a shock wave as the plane breaks the sound barrier. This makes a loud bang.

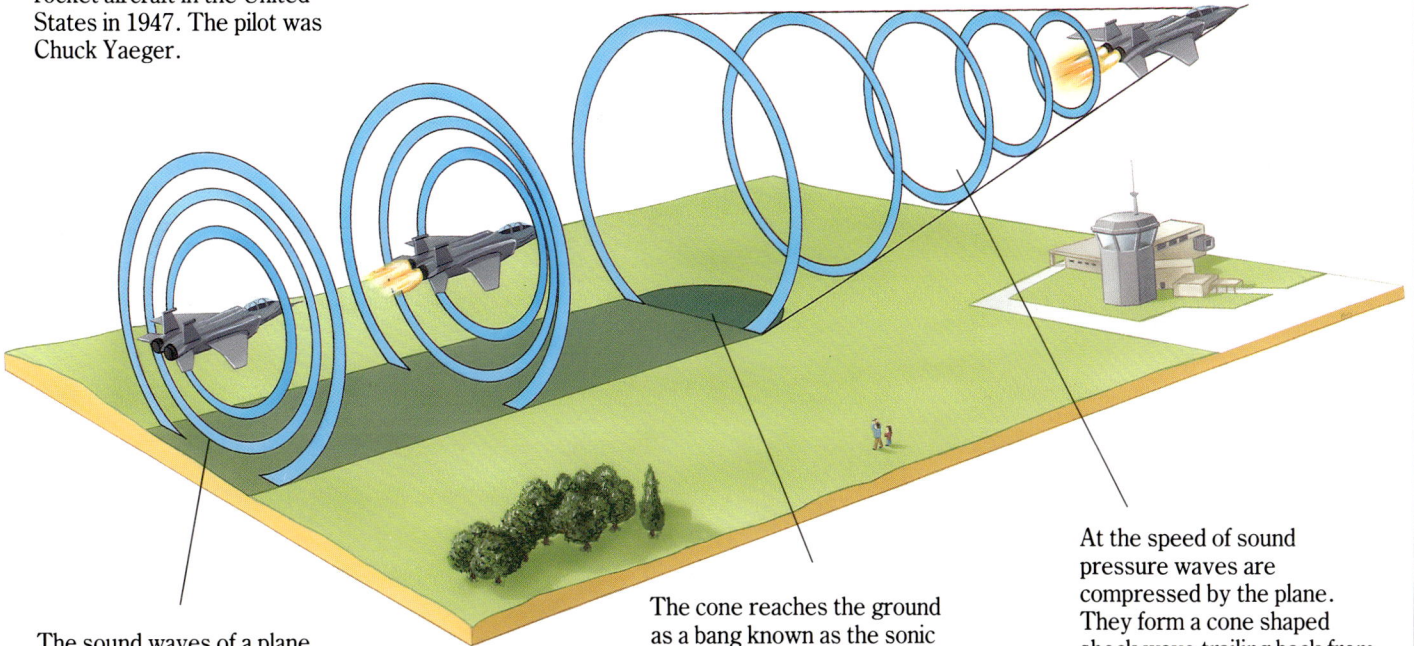

The first plane to break the sound barrier was the Bell X-1 rocket aircraft in the United States in 1947. The pilot was Chuck Yaeger.

The sound waves of a plane flying slower than sound spread out like the ripples on a pond. As it flies faster it begins to catch up with the sound it makes.

The cone reaches the ground as a bang known as the sonic boom. The shock waves of a sonic boom can break windows. The nose and tail of a plane can create separate shock waves making a double sonic boom.

At the speed of sound pressure waves are compressed by the plane. They form a cone shaped shock wave trailing back from the plane.

Hertz

Heinrich Hertz (1857–1894) was the first person to broadcast and receive radio waves. He gave his name to the Hertz (Hz), the unit used for the frequency of sound waves.

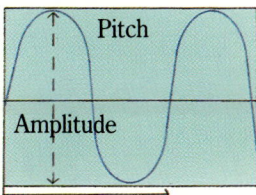

Pitch

Amplitude

FREQUENCY

The number of vibrations a sound makes in a second is called the frequency. Frequency is measured in hertz (Hz), and one hertz means one vibration per second. The dial of a radio is full of wavelengths measured in hertz. The lowest note a person can hear is 20 Hz and the highest is 20,000 Hz.

Pitch and amplitude

The pitch of a sound is to do with the speed at which an object vibrates. The higher the frequency the higher the pitch. Amplitude measures the distance of a radio wave from its highest point to its lowest point.

Bat up to 120,000 Hz

Dolphin up to 110,000 Hz

Dog up to 50,000 Hz

Human up to 20,000 Hz

Cricket up to 15,000 Hz

Different animals hear different frequencies.

How bright the Sun is?

Candela
The brightness of light is measured in candelas.

Newton and the prism
Light is really a range of colours, the spectrum. Isaac Newton (1642–1727) used a prism to bend white light and separate the colours.

The Sun is a star, which means that it is a huge ball of gas so hot it creates a nuclear reaction. That reaction provides the light and warmth essential for all life on Earth. The Sun even made coal and oil because these are the remains of plants and animals. Many people have worshipped it as a god. It will burn out eventually, but not for thousands of millions of years.

The Sun
Light from the Sun takes just over eight minutes to reach Earth. The temperature at its centre is about sixteen million °C. It burns up 4000 million tons of gas every second, but there's plenty left. Its mass is 333,000 times greater than Earth's and it could hold a million Earths inside it. It shoots out tiny particles which take two days to reach Earth and interfere with radio signals.

THE ELECTROMAGNETIC SPECTRUM
Energy can also move in wavelengths that are invisible to us. It is called the electromagnetic spectrum. The distance from one crest of a wave to the next is the wavelength. The number of waves reaching a fixed point in a second is the frequency. Radio waves have the longest frequency and cosmic rays have the shortest. They all travel at the speed of light.

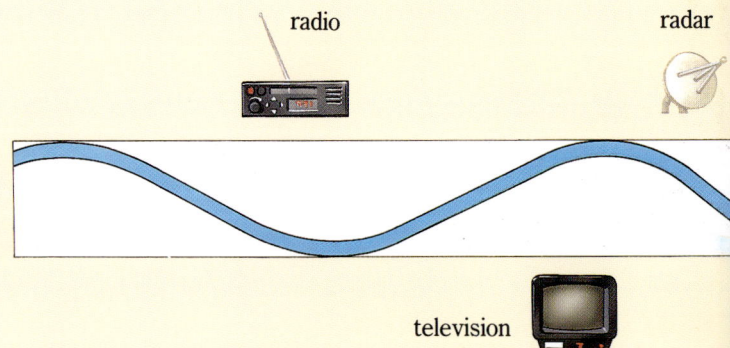

radio

radar

television

Speed of light
Light travels at 299,000 km (186,000 miles) per second. If you were able to travel at that speed you would be able to go round the world seven and a half times in a second.

Einstein
According to Albert Einstein's theory of relativity nothing can travel faster than light, and light always passes you at the same relative speed whether you are moving very fast or not.

A stationary star would send out a steady wavelength of light which would be in the middle of the spectrum.

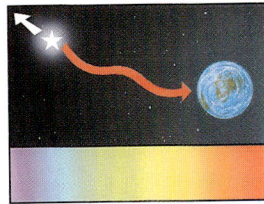

A receding star sends out a longer wavelength of light which has shifted towards the red end of the spectrum.

Red shift
Astronomers have noticed that the light coming from stars, when split into a spectrum, is redder than they expected. The light has been shifted to the red lower end of the spectrum. This means that the stars are travelling away from the Earth and the solar system and that the universe is expanding.

Maxwell
A Scottish scientist, James Maxwell (1831–1879), was the first to realise that electricity and magnetism are connected. He discovered that changes in electrical current generate electromagnetic waves. His experiments revealed that light is made up of electromagnetic waves moving incredibly fast.

infrared

visible light

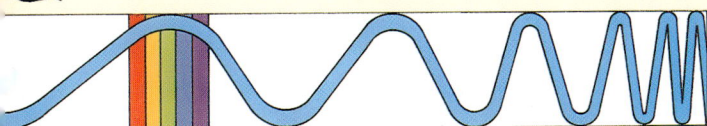

X-rays

Gamma rays

ultraviolet

microwaves

Light years
When you look at the stars you are seeing virtually all of them as they were before you were born. The distances across space are too vast to be measured in normal ways. They are measured in light years, the distance light travels in a year. In a year light travels 9.5 million million km (5.9 million million miles). Light from the nearest star to the Sun takes four years to reach us, and from distant stars it takes millions of years.

How to measure angles?

A ny measurement of land or buildings depends on angles. They are divided into degrees. A complete turn of a circle is 360 degrees. A quarter of a circle and the corner of a square are 90 degrees. When sailors travel out of sight of land they need some means of calculating where they are. Navigational instruments do this by measuring the angles of the Sun and stars.

Pythagoras

Pythagoras (582–497 BC) discovered a key aspect of angles. His theorem says that in a right angled triangle the square on the *hypotoneuse* is equal to the sum of the squares on the other two sides.

Angles of elevation

In this engraving published in Germany in 1547 two gunners are calculating *elevation*. The one on the left is using a *clinometer* which measures the angle of a slope. The other is using a *quadrant*.

Ballistics

People used to think that a cannonball flew in a straight line until it was over the target and then dropped straight down. Galileo studied ballistics and showed that gravity acts on the cannonball so it flies in a curve known as a parabola. The name ballistics comes from ballista, a machine for hurling stones and spears.

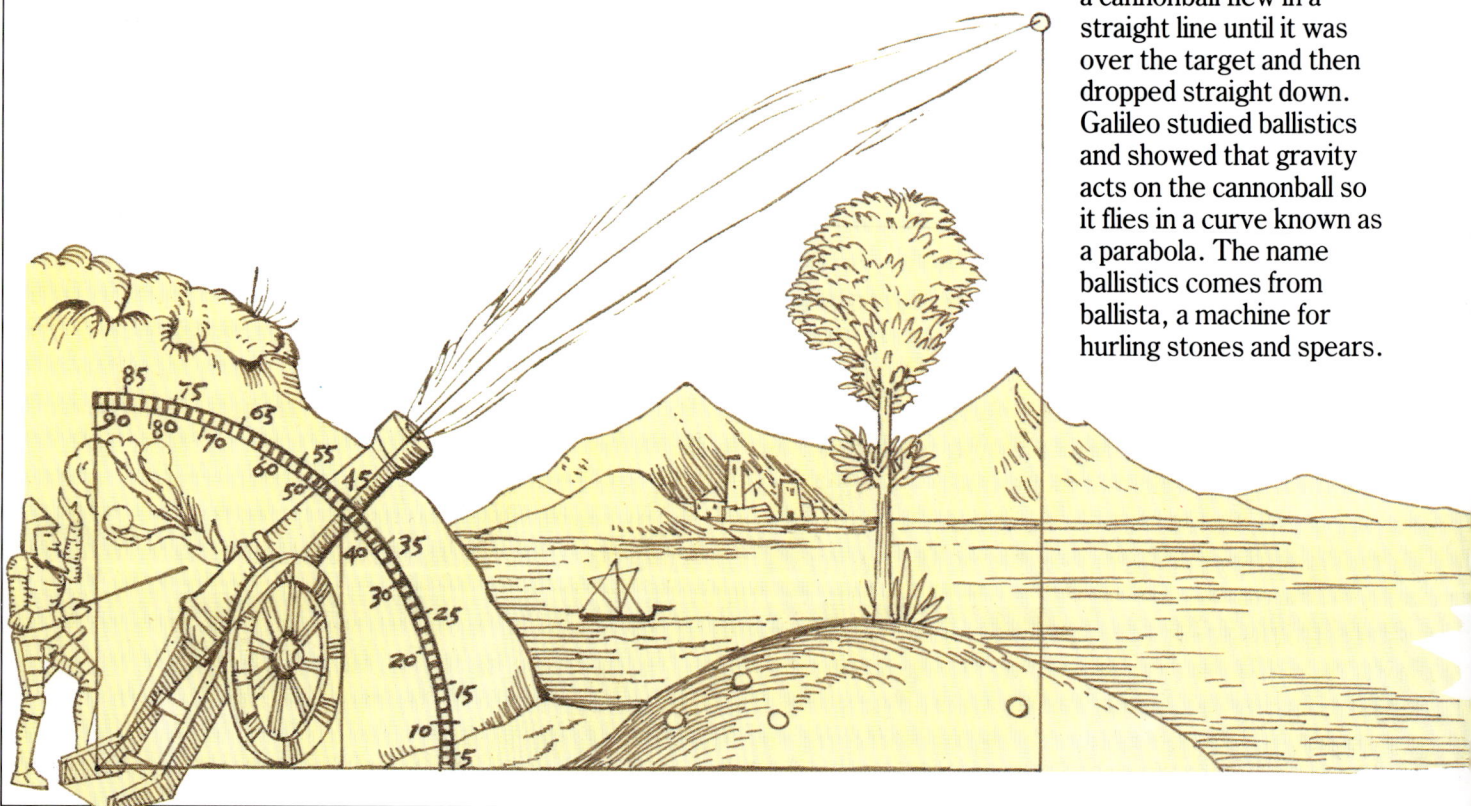

Astrolabe

The astrolabe is a two-dimensional model of the sky used to calculate the angles of the Sun, Moon and stars and indicate distances and direction.

Astrolabe

Quadrant to octant

The quadrant measured the position of stars to calculate latitude. The octant was an improved version of it made in 1730 which used mirrors to align a star and the *horizon*.

A sailor sighting through a sextant.

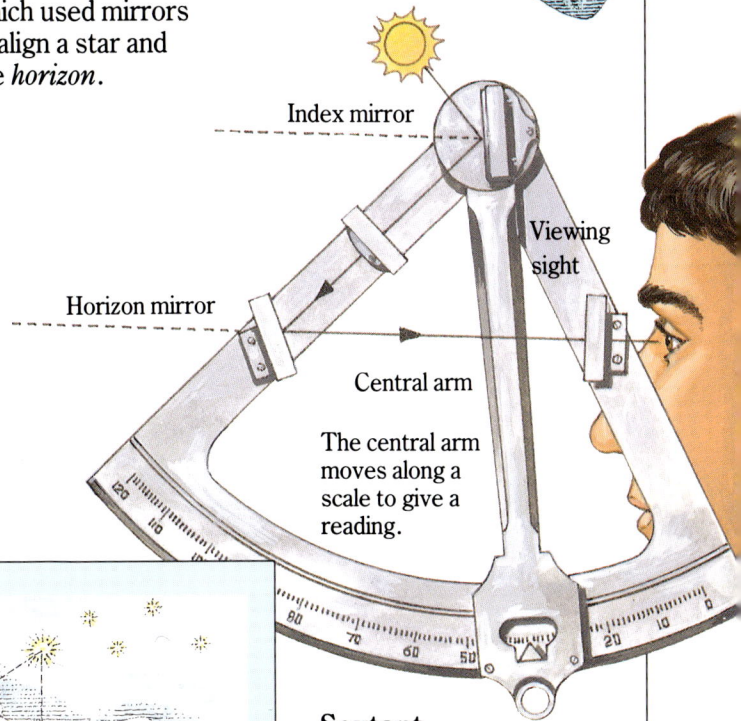

Index mirror

Viewing sight

Horizon mirror

Central arm

The central arm moves along a scale to give a reading.

Crosstaff

A navigator placed the end of the crosstaff against an eye and moved the crosspiece until one end lined up with the horizon and the other with a star. A scale on the staff helped calculate latitude.

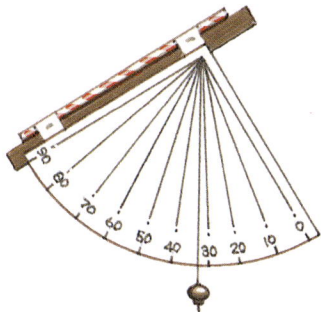

Measuring elevation

This scale measures the angle of elevation. A sighting is taken along the upper edge to the topmost point of the house or tree or whatever feature is being used in the survey. The angle between the horizon and the topmost point is the angle of elevation.

Sextant

The sextant soon replaced the octant. It works on the same principle and uses mirrors, telescope and moveable arms to measure latitude with great accuracy. It is still in use today.

TRIANGULATION AND THEODOLITES

Land surveying involves a *three dimensional* measurement of all the features in the area being surveyed. A surveyor uses triangulation, measuring a network of triangles across the land because this gives great accuracy. More triangles can be measured from the three points of the first triangle. A theodolite is like a telescope which measures angles horizontally and vertically. Many hills in Britain have concrete pillars on top called triangulation points. A surveyor can take the theodolite off its tripod and mount it on the pillar to measure anything in sight.

Glossary

Air Resistance.
The action of air opposing or resisting the movement of any object through it.

Axis.
Imaginary line about which the Earth rotates.

Barometer.
An instrument which measures atmospheric pressure. Changes in pressure help to predict changes in weather.

Clinometer.
An instrument for measuring slopes and elevations.

Currents.
The flow of substances, like water, air or electricity, in one direction.

Density.
The degree to which the matter of a substance or object is crowded together.

Displacement.
The act of pushing a fluid aside by the same volume as an object placed in it.

Elevation.
The angle of something compared to the horizon.

Evaporation.
The conversion of a liquid into a vapour.

Frequency.
The rate at which something repeats.

Geothermal.
Heat below the Earth's surface.

Hebrew.
Another name for Jew, and for the Jewish language.

Horizon.
The line at which the Earth and sky appear to meet.

Hydroelectric.
The use of water power to generate electricity.

Hypoteneuse.
The name for the side of a triangle opposite to the right angle.

Greenwich Meridian Line.
An imaginary line of longitude from pole to pole which passes through Greenwich, east of London.

Levers.
Bars of metal used to move objects.

Mass.
The amount of matter contained in an object.

Medium.
The intervening substance through which a force acts on objects.

Metrication.
The application and use of the metric system of measurements.

Molecules.
The groups of atoms which form the basic chemical units of substances.

Orbit.
The curved path taken by an object in space round a larger object, for example the Earth round the Sun.

Photosynthesis.
The conversion of light by green plants into energy.

Pressure.
The application of a continuous force on a body.

Quadrant.
A quarter of a day, or of a circle.

Radioactive.
Energy in the form of rays and particles which are thrown off at high velocity from some materials.

Renaissance.
It means rebirth and describes the great developments in art and learning which began in Italy in the fifteenth and sixteenth centuries.

Royal Society.
A gathering of scientists in Britain which began in 1645 with the purpose of expanding scientific knowledge.

Shock Waves.
The sudden and rapid movement of air compressed by a plane as it reaches the speed of sound. It can be heard as a sonic boom.

Speed of Light.
Light travels at 299,000 kph (186,000 miles per hour), and it is believed nothing travels faster.

Standardise.
To make things conform to a uniform size, weight or shape.

Surveyor.
A person who examines and inspects land or structures.

Theodolite.
A surveying instrument, similar to a telescope, for measuring angles.

Theory of Evolution.
The development of a species from earlier forms through natural selection in order to survive.

Three Dimensional.
Objects such as cubes, spheres and pyramids which have length, breadth and thickness.

Transformer.
An apparatus for increasing or decreasing the electric force to the level at which it is needed.

Vacuum.
A completely empty space which doesn't even contain air.

Index